Person centred approaches when supporting people with a learning disability

Series Editor: Lesley Barcham

Mandatory unit and Common Induction Standards titles

Communicating effectively with people with a learning disability
ISBN 978 0 85725 510 5

Personal development for learning disability workers ISBN 978 0 85725 609 6

Equality and inclusion for learning disability workers ISBN 978 0 85725 514 3

Duty of care for learning disability workers ISBN 978 0 85725 613 3

Principles of safeguarding and protection for learning disability workers
ISBN 978 0 85725 506 8

Person centred approaches when supporting people with a learning disability
ISBN 978 0 85725 625 6

The role of the learning disability worker ISBN 978 0 85725 637 9

Person centred approaches when supporting people with a learning disability

Liz Tilly

Supporting the level 2 and 3 Diplomas in
Health and Social Care (learning disability pathway)
and the Common Induction Standards

all about people

Los Angeles | London | New Delhi
Singapore | Washington DC

Acknowledgements

Photographs from www.crocodilehouse.co.uk, www.careimages.com, www.thepowerofpostiveimages.com and www.shutterstock.com

Our thanks to Marie, Marianne and Sophie, and to Choices Housing for their help.

First published in 2011 jointly by Learning Matters Ltd and the British Institute of Learning Disabilities
Reprinted 2012

British Library Cataloguing in Publication Data
A CIP record for this book is available from the British Library

ISBN: 978 0 85725 625 6

This book is also available in the following ebook formats:
Adobe ebook ISBN: 978 0 85725 627 0
EPUB ebook ISBN: 978 0 85725 626 3
Kindle ISBN: 978 0 85725 628 7

The right of Liz Tilly to be identified as the author of this Work has been asserted by her in accordance with the Copyright, Designs and Patents Act 1988.

Cover design by Pentacor
Text design by Pentacor
Project Management by Deer Park Productions, Tavistock
Typeset by Pantek Arts Ltd, Maidstone
Printed and bound in Great Britain by Ashford Colour Press Ltd, Gosport, Hants

Learning Matters
An imprint of SAGE Publications Ltd
1 Oliver's Yard
55 City Road
London EC1Y 1SP

SAGE Publications Inc.
2455 Teller Road
Thousand Oaks, California 91320

SAGE Publications India Pvt Ltd
B 1/I 1 Mohan Cooperative Industrial Area
Mathura Road
New Delhi 110 044

SAGE Publications Asia-Pacific Pte Ltd
3 Church Street
#10–04 Samsung Hub
Singapore 049483

BILD
Campion House
Green Street
Kidderminster
Worcestershire
DY10 1JL
Tel: 01562 723010
E-mail: enquiries@bild.org.uk
www.bild.org.uk

MIX
Paper from
responsible sources
FSC® C011748

Contents

This book covers:

- Common Induction Standards – Standard 7 – Person centred support
- Level 2 and Level 3 diploma units HSC 026 – Implementing person centred approaches in health and social care and HSC 036 – Promote person centred approaches in health and social care

Liz Tilly

Liz is strongly committed to the full inclusion of people with learning disabilities in all aspects of life, and has had regular professional and social contact with people with learning disabilities for over 30 years.

Liz works as a freelance trainer and consultant and also set up and is a director of Building Bridges Training, a social enterprise of people with a learning disability which provides training. Liz founded and was chief executive of a voluntary organisation in the West Midlands which provides a wide range of services and opportunities for people with learning disabilities. Prior to this, her career was in special education.

She has learning disability qualifications including a B.Ed. and M.Med.Sci. and a M.A. in Applied Social Research. She is currently doing a Ph.D. researching the needs of and support to people with mild learning disabilities who fall through the net of statutory provision.

Introduction

Who is this book for?

Person Centred Approaches when Supporting People with a Learning Disability is for you if you:

- have a new job working with people with learning disabilities with a support provider or as a personal assistant;

- are a more experienced worker who is studying for a qualification for your own professional development or are seeking more information to improve your practice;

- are a volunteer supporting people with a learning disability;

- are a manager in a service supporting people with a learning disability and you have training or supervisory responsibility for the induction of new workers and the continuous professional development of more experienced staff;

- if you are a direct payment or personal budget user and are planning the induction or training for your personal assistant.

Links to qualifications and the Common Induction Standards

This book gives you all the information you need to complete both one of the Common Induction Standards and the unit on person centred approaches when supporting people with a learning disability from the level 2 and level 3 diplomas in health and social care. You may use the learning from this unit in a number of ways:

- to help you complete the Common Induction Standards;

- to work towards a full qualification e.g. the level 2 or level 3 diploma in health and social care;

- as learning for the unit on person centred support for your professional development.

This unit is one of the mandatory units that everyone doing the full level 2 and level 3 diploma must study. Although anyone studying for the qualifications will find the book useful, it is particularly helpful for people who support a person with a learning disability. The messages and stories used in this book are from people with a learning disability, family carers and people working with them.

Links to assessment

If you are studying for this unit and want to gain accreditation towards a qualification, first of all you will need to make sure that you are registered with an awarding organisation who offers the qualification. Then you will need to provide a portfolio of evidence for assessment. The person responsible for training within your organisation will advise you about registering with an awarding organisation and give you information about the type of evidence you will need to provide for assessment. You can also get additional information from BILD. For more information about qualifications and assessment, please go to the BILD website: www.bild.org.uk/qualifications

How this book is organised

Generally each chapter covers one learning outcome from the qualification unit, and one of the Common Induction Standards. The learning outcomes covered are clearly highlighted at the beginning of each chapter. Each chapter starts with a story from a person with a learning disability or family carer or worker. This introduces the topic and is intended to help you think about the topic from their point of view. Each chapter contains:

 Thinking points – to help you reflect on your practice;

Stories – examples of good support from people with learning disabilities and family carers;

 Activities – for you to use to help you to think about your work with people with learning disabilities;

Key points – a summary of the main messages in that chapter;

References and where to go for more information – useful references to help further study.

At the end of the book there is:

A glossary – explaining specialist language in plain English;

An index – to help you look up a particular topic easily.

Study skills

Studying for a qualification can be very rewarding. However, it can be daunting if you have not studied for a long time, or are wondering how to fit your studies into an already busy life. The BILD website contains lots of advice to help you to study successfully, including information about effective reading, taking notes, organising your time, using the internet for research. For further information, go to www.bild.org.uk/qualifications

Chapter 1

Understanding person centred approaches when supporting people with a learning disability

> Good support for me is different every day. Listen to me. Help me to have a good day. One day it might be about money, shopping and paying the bills, the next day it's about keeping the house clean and going to volunteer at the centre. On another day if I am poorly then it's about my support worker ringing for the doctor. If it's a cold it's easy, but if not it could be the hospital!
>
> *Sandra gets support to live the life she chooses in her own flat, spending her time as a volunteer and going out on local shopping trips and to see friends and family.*

Introduction

People with learning disabilities should be at the centre of all decision-making that affects their life. Putting the individual's needs and choices at the centre of the care and support you provide is often referred to as using a person centred approach in the way you work.

As a support worker you will need to find out about the history, preferences, wishes and needs of the person you support and to use this information to influence the day-to-day support you provide. In services for people with learning disabilities we refer to this as person centred planning and support. Simply put, it is a way of asking what people want, what support they need and how they can get it. It assists people to live an independent and inclusive life.

Learning outcomes

This chapter will help you to:

- explain person centred values and how they must influence all aspects of your work;
- understand the importance of working in a person centred way with people with learning disabilities;

- understand the role of risk taking in person centred support;
- explain how a care plan will help you work in a person centred way;
- evaluate the use of care plans in applying person centred values.

This chapter covers:

- Common Induction Standards – Standard 7 – Person centred support: Learning Outcome 1
- Level 2 HSC 026 – Implement person centred approaches in health and social care: Learning Outcome 1
- Level 3 HSC 036 – Promote person centred approaches in health and social care: Learning Outcome 1

Person centred values and how to apply them in your work

First, we need to explore what each of the following values means in practice in your everyday work when supporting people who have learning disabilities. You will notice that these values do not stand alone but are closely related to each other, for example choice and independence, respect and dignity. These values are the foundations of the day-to-day support you provide to people with learning disabilities. You should think about how you apply them in your work each day.

1. Choice

Every day we make many choices. All choices are important even though some of them are quite small and others can be more far reaching. Day-to-day choices are often about the clothes we wear, the food we eat, how we spend our money and who we spend time with. Other choices we make include where to work, who to live with, where to live and where to go on holiday. We take the freedom to make these choices for granted, but they are often made for people with learning disabilities without regard for their wishes.

Choice is not only for people who can speak for themselves. People with severe or profound learning disabilities can make many choices for themselves. You will need to develop your observation skills to look out for ways that the person you support expresses their preferences. Over time you will be able to build up a more detailed understanding of how they communicate their likes and dislikes. You can then use this information to involve the person in making more choices.

Having choice over a particular part of our life means we have control and it is good for our emotional and mental health. In your day-to-day role as a support worker this involves:

- ensuring that people with learning disabilities are fully included in making choices and taking decisions about their own life;

- supporting people by making sure they have enough information to make choices, in a form they can understand;

- supporting people when they speak up for themselves, even if they do not communicate in words.

Choice means having access to a wide range of options and information, knowing the advantages and disadvantages of each, deciding for yourself which ones suit you best and having your choice respected and supported.

2. Privacy

Privacy is a basic human need. We all need to do some things alone and have time to ourselves to do as we please. Our need for privacy depends on our personality, interests and circumstances. You must respect people's need for privacy whenever it arises. If your work involves supporting a person with their personal care you will need to make particular efforts to ensure privacy for them.

It's really important to Joe to spend time in his room. He likes to copy from his books and magazines and listen to his music and he enjoys time on his own. Once a well meaning support worker tried to encourage him to spend more time with the two other people in the home, but later realised working hard all day at the gardening project meant that he needed time alone to 'recharge his batteries'.

Activity

Think about what privacy means for you. Would you describe yourself as someone who needs a lot of privacy? What about the person you support? Talk to your manager about privacy and the practical ways that you can ensure people get the privacy they need.

3. Independence

None of us are truly independent, however much we may wish to be. We are dependent on other people for many aspects of our daily life – the supply of electricity and water to our home, the food we eat and the transport we use, not to mention access to communications such as phones, TV and the internet. More importantly, we are dependent on those close to us for their love, support and affection. It is more accurate to say that we are all interdependent. We need other people in all areas of our life.

Although people with learning disabilities are taking more control of their lives, they are all too often on the receiving end of other people's decisions and planning. They may not have the power or control to decide their own lifestyle. Other people – service providers, families or support workers – can often make these decisions for them. Others may be well supported but lack the confidence or experience to take control of their lives.

You have a vitally important role in the empowerment of people with learning disabilities to become independent. You can't empower them yourself – people can only empower themselves – but you can help them to work towards independence. This can't happen overnight, especially for people who have been dependent and disempowered all their lives. It is a process which happens step by step and will take people with learning disabilities some time to achieve.

4. Dignity

People with learning disabilities have the same rights as every other citizen in our society. This fundamental principle means that people with learning disabilities should never be treated in an inhumane or degrading way, but should always be treated courteously as people of value in their own right. You should always seek to maintain the dignity of each person you work with. Occasionally, this may mean discouraging a person from doing something that would cause them embarrassment or humiliation.

You can promote dignity by listening to people when they express their needs and wants.

Dignity means that we recognise and value people with learning disabilities as equal citizens with the same rights as everyone else. By showing dignity in your everyday actions you can reinforce this idea for the person concerned and for others who see how you support them. For more information about promoting dignity go to The Dignity Challenge website: www.dignityincare.org.uk

Activity

The Dignity Challenge is made up of ten statements. Discuss the ten statements below with your line manager or an experienced colleague. Think of three ways that you promote dignity in your day-to-day work.

- *Have a zero tolerance of all forms of abuse.*
- *Support people with the same respect you would want for yourself or a member of your family.*
- *Treat each person as an individual by offering a personalised service.*
- *Enable people to maintain the maximum possible level of independence, choice and control.*
- *Listen and support people to express their needs and wants.*
- *Respect people's right to privacy.*
- *Ensure people feel able to complain without fear of retribution.*
- *Engage with family members and carers as care partners.*
- *Assist people to maintain confidence and positive self-esteem.*
- *Act to alleviate people's loneliness and isolation.*

5. Respect

The way that you and your colleagues behave towards the people with learning disabilities you support will affect the way that other people see them and the way they see themselves. You should always show consideration to the people with learning disability that you work with, and demonstrate through your actions and attitudes that everyone is worthy of respect.

Respect means behaving towards people with the consideration they deserve, showing that you value their opinions, views and achievements no matter how different these may be from your own. Respect means taking greater care to be aware of what the person feels and understands, as far as possible.

Thinking point

Respect has become a rather well used word in the media and by politicians. What does 'being respected' mean to the people with a learning disability and the family carers you work with? How do you show respect in your day-to-day work with them?

6. Partnership

Every day in your work as a learning disability worker you are a partner with the person with a learning disability you support. You are working with them so that they can fulfil their dreams and ambitions and you can assist them with their particular needs.

Partnership also involves other people working together so that the needs of people with learning disabilities are met as fully as possible. The family of the person with learning disabilities you support are often very important partners in your work. Most family carers have a wealth of knowledge and experience about their family member, their likes and dislikes, their personal history and any particular medical needs and are more than happy to share what they know with new workers.

It is important to remember that when we ask family carers for information, most families have seen many workers come and go in their relative's life and they may have repeated information very many times. Some may feel disillusioned because of past experiences when things have not changed as they had hoped.

Important characteristics of partnership working that you need to develop include:

- focusing with partners on your shared commitment to the person you support;
- always seeking to understand why different partners need each other;
- agreeing on your goals and objectives in working together;
- working to develop and sustain trust in each other;
- demonstrating you are committed to the partnership;
- communicating regularly and effectively with partners on the work you are doing together.

7. Equality

Thinking point

What do you think equality means for a person you know who has a learning disability?

Discrimination against people with learning disabilities and their families often results in the unfair and unequal treatment of people solely on account of that learning disability. They may not be allowed the freedom and opportunities which the Equality Act (2010) and other laws promote. People with learning disabilities often face prejudice and discrimination and may be treated unequally and unjustly and denied the opportunities which should be available to them, just as they are to other citizens.

Equality means that people with learning disabilities should:

- no longer be marginalised and isolated within society;
- have the same social status as other people;
- no longer be subject to exploitation and abuse;
- have their opinions taken seriously;
- have their adult status recognised;
- have the same citizenship rights as other people.

Failure to give equality to people with learning disabilities denies our common humanity, causes anger, frustration, despair, helplessness and loneliness for the people involved, and keeps them powerless and dependent.

8. Individuality

Everyone you work with is an individual with their own particular likes, dislikes, strengths and personality. Services and support workers should always focus on the individuals they are working with rather than on the needs of a group of people. You and your colleagues should have the hopes, dreams, interests and needs of each person you support as a top priority in your daily work. See Chapter 6 for more about supporting people's wellbeing and identity.

9. Rights

The rights of people with learning disabilities as citizens are protected by law and in particular by the Human Rights Act (1998). People with learning disabilities who are supported by health and social care organisations are protected by the rights included in the Act.

Sixteen basic human rights have been incorporated into UK law. These rights protect us from harm and set out what we can say and do as well as our right to a fair trial and other basic entitlements. The rights are:

- right to life;
- prohibition of torture;
- prohibition of slavery and forced labour;
- right to liberty and security;
- right to a fair trial;
- no punishment without law;
- right to respect for private and family life;
- freedom of thought, conscience and religion;
- freedom of expression;
- freedom of assembly and association;
- right to marry;
- prohibition of discrimination;
- protection of property;
- right to education;
- right to free elections;
- abolition of the death penalty.

There are short, easy read guides available for both the UN Declaration on Human Rights and the Human Rights Act at:

- www.equalityhumanrights.com
- www.justice.gov.uk
- www.equalities.gov.uk

You have an important role in upholding people's rights and in showing others in the community how to support people with learning disabilities.

Gateway, which was once the part of Mencap that provided social and leisure opportunities, also developed a set of rights with their members. These are the rights that people with a learning disability have said are important to them:

- the right to be yourself;
- the right to be treated with dignity and respect;

- the right to form relationships and develop sexuality;
- the right to privacy;
- the right to look ahead and help decide what will happen;
- the right to make informed decisions and have choices;
- the right to take informed risks and make mistakes;
- the right to get involved in the community;
- the right to be and the right to feel;
- the right to speak up for yourself;
- the right to get information.

We all have the right to a private and family life, and to marry.

Gateway go on to say that we need to accept that with every right there is also an individual responsibility. Many local self-advocacy groups and organisations have developed a similar set of rights.

There is more information on the Human Rights Act, the Equality Act and the areas of inclusion and rights in the book in this series by Rorie Fulton and Kate Richardson, *Equality and Inclusion for Learning Disability Workers*.

The importance of person centred working with people with a learning disability

Working in a person centred way with people with a learning disability is essential in your role as a support worker because:

- the *Code of Practice for Social Care Workers* says you must 'protect the rights and promote the interests of service users and carers' and 'respect and maintain the dignity and privacy of service users';

- you must always work within the law on human rights and equality and take account of the government policies for the country that you live in;

- there are a number of government policies that specifically support and promote person centred working and support.

Government policies on supporting people with a learning disability

Recent government policies have promoted the development of person centred services and support for all people who receive health and social care support. They focus on people having more choice, control and independence and services being more person centred.

The table below lists the main learning disability policy documents for the four countries in the UK. All of them endorse the principles of person centred support and the delivery of person centred services. They are all available in an easy read format as well as the full version.

Valuing People: A new strategy for learning disability for the 21st century and *Valuing People Now: A three year strategy for people with learning disabilities*	Department of Health (2001 and 2009)	England
The Same as You? A review of services for people with learning disabilities	Scottish Executive (2000)	Scotland

Equal Lives: Review of policy and services for people with a learning disability in Northern Ireland	Department of Health and Social Services and Public Safety (2005)	Northern Ireland
Statement on Policy and Practice for Adults with a Learning Disability	Welsh Assembly Government (2007)	Wales

In the White Paper *Valuing People* (2001) the government clearly spelled out their priority for services in England:

'A person-centred approach… means that planning should start with the individual (not with the service), and take account of their wishes and aspirations.'

Valuing People Now (2009) is the government's three year strategy to improve the lives of people with learning disabilities and their families. It covers all aspects of life, including health, housing, getting a paid job, personalisation, transition, advocacy, hate crime and relationships.

Valuing People Now says that all people with learning disabilities and their families should have greater choice and control over their lives. This means that local authorities, health and other service providers need to reshape and redesign their systems to give people with learning disabilities and their families more control over the support they receive.

The policy for Wales, the *Statement on Policy and Practice for Adults with a Learning Disability* (2007), similarly says: 'That local services should be shaped by the users of services and their needs lies at the heart of the Welsh Assembly Government's strategic approach. Individual planning approaches are fundamental to achieving this aim and to establishing a collaborative approach between adults with a learning disability, their family and all professionals involved in providing support.'

Government policies on personalisation

Recently the term personalisation has been used to mean wider changes to social care so that the whole system of delivering support is person centred. This has been set out in several government policies including *Putting People First* (2007), *Think Local Act Personal* (2011) and *A Vision for Adult Social Care* (2010).

Recently there has been a growth in person centred support for people with learning disabilities through the use of direct payments and individual budgets.

Some of these changes have been led by national organisations such as In Control, a social enterprise that was set up to transform the current social care system into a system of self-directed support. In Control supports local authorities and other organisations to implement self-directed support. You can find out more at www.in-control.org.uk and www.thinklocalactpersonal.org.uk

In recent years direct payments and individual budgets have been the main ways that people needing social care support have been able to direct or manage their support in a person centred way.

- **Direct payments** are local council payments for people who have been assessed as needing social care support and who would like to arrange their own care and support services instead of receiving them directly from the local council. People can receive support to manage their direct payment from family or friends or from user-led organisations.

- **Individual budget or self-directed support** is a process that is directly controlled by the person who receives the funding for their support, following an assessment of their needs. Self-directed support means the person can make their own decision about the support and services they need. Self-directed support starts by looking at the person and defining what support they need to lead a fulfilling life and what natural support they already have from family and friends.

You can find more information about how people with a learning disability have used direct payments and individual budgets on the In Control website, at www.in-control.org.uk and on the Social Care Institute for Excellence website, at www.scie.org.uk

The role of risk taking in person centred support

Risk is part of everyday life. In your role as a learning disability worker you need to work with the person you support to help them lead the life they want. Working in a person centred way doesn't mean that you should be seeking to eliminate all the risks. Rather you should be working with the person to identify and manage risks. Planned and managed risk is an essential part of person centred support. This is covered fully in Chapter 7.

How a care plan can help you work in a person centred way

Care plans, health action plans, person centred plans, support plans – what's the difference?

It can be very confusing when you hear all these different names. This section will explain what is generally understood by the different labels, but you may need to check what words and meanings are used in your organisation for the different plans people have. What is important at the end of the day is that the person has a plan that informs others about what support they need and want, how it is delivered and their dreams and aspirations.

A person centred plan

Person centred planning is a structured way for a person to plan their lives, and for those who provide services to understand and work towards the dreams, aspirations and needs of the people they support. The person centred plan is a record of the person centred planning process, which is about identifying what people need and want now and in the future. A person centred plan can be developed by using person centred planning tools.

There are six main people centred planning tools used in the UK:

- Essential Lifestyle Planning;
- Personal Futures Planning;
- Individual Service Design;
- PATH (Planning Alternative Tomorrows with Hope);
- MAP (Making Actions Happen);
- Circles of support.

The references at the end of this chapter will help you if you want to find more information.

Person centred planning helps people plan their lives.

A support plan

A support plan may refer to two types of plans in learning disabilities services:

1. The term is used by people who have an individual budget. It links the person centred plan with the amount of money they have been allocated in their budget, and describes how the support will be arranged and how the person will stay in control. The local authority has to agree to the support plan as the trigger for providing the money to the person. It is important that the support plan is more than just about how support and care will be delivered but still includes the important things to the person, such as what they like to do for a treat at the weekend, and what their plans are for the future.

2. In addition, if you support a person with complex needs who finds it difficult to communicate the details of their care, there should be an additional document as part of the person centred plan which outlines the specific day-to-day support a person needs and how it should be delivered. This can be called a support plan. You need to know what your organisation calls them and where they are kept, and how they are updated. Although this document is for the benefit of staff, it is also important to ensure it is person centred.

A care plan

In most services, support plans and person centred plans are gradually replacing care plans for people with learning disabilities. In the past, care plans referred to the type of plan we had before person centred planning came to be recognised as the way forward. It was typically a plan written by staff with a focus on the service and the budget and was kept in a filing cabinet in the manager's office. The person was usually referred to as the 'service user' or 'client' in the plan. Sometimes care plans focused on what people couldn't do and their disabilities and health problems. They often included basic assessments of skills and needs rather than addressing people's hopes and dreams for the future. Single episodes of challenging behaviour or a refusal to follow staff requests would lead to people being labelled as having a bad reputation.

Some organisations may still use the term care plan, but what matters at the end of the day is that the plan is developed around the needs of the person, with them participating in its creation and able to understand the way it is recorded.

Health action plans

Many people with a learning disability may also have a health action plan which sets out the things they can do to stay healthy and who can help them with their health needs. Many people develop their plan with their doctor or another health worker who supports them. The health action plan should be kept by the person and regularly updated to take account of any changing health needs.

How a plan helps you to work in a person centred way

Person centred planning is different from other approaches to planning and it can help you work in a person centred way because:

- it focuses on the positive aspects of the person;
- the person with a learning disability, or where appropriate a family carer, is in charge of the process;
- professionals are partners in the process along with the other people invited by the individual;

- there is an emphasis on finding new and creative ways of solving problems and creating ways of achieving what the person wants;
- the stress is on interdependence rather than making the person independent.

All of these qualities should be reflected in the way you work from day to day.

The five key features of person centred ways of working

1. **The person is at the centre of the process**. This is about really listening to the person concerned, learning about the person and understanding their talents, strengths and aspirations. It is about strengthening the person's voice. It involves a commitment to sharing power with the person.

2. **Individual rights, independence and choice are essential**. Person centred working is a rights-based process. Without recognition of the individual's full rights as a citizen and human being, it cannot work.

3. **Family members and friends are full partners**. Power sharing involves not only the person but also family members, friends and other significant people in the person's life. The person at the centre and those who are important to that person take the lead role in deciding what opportunities need to be created and what support is required. This involves rethinking and reshaping the role of the professional and an acknowledgement that the professionals no longer have control, but are partners in the problem-solving process.

4. **Autonomy and interdependence are important**. Autonomy means running your own life and making your own decisions. However, we all live alongside others who have rights equal to our own. Interdependence means people are not seen only as individuals, but as individuals within the context of their families and communities.

5. **Individual capabilities should be recognised**. Person centred working focuses on a person's capabilities, the things that are important to that person and the support the person needs. The things people can do are more important than what they can't do.

Thinking point

Take one of the five key features of person centred working above and reflect on how you have put this idea into practice in the last week.

Evaluating the use of plans in supporting people with learning disabilities

Person centred plans are essential to enabling people to have person centred support, as it means everyone is working to the end goals that the person has chosen and all workers support the person as set out in their plan.

But a plan won't be able to make the person's dreams become a reality unless it is implemented. This means putting the plan into practice for everyone involved, including staff, family, friends and professionals.

You can evaluate the person's care plan or support plan by questioning it:

- Does the plan clearly describe the person in a positive way?

- Does the plan clearly describe the person's hopes and dreams?

- Does the plan clearly say who will provide support, and in what areas, to enable the plan to become reality?

- Do people provide feedback on how the support has been carried out?

- Is the plan regularly reviewed and are all the key people involved in the review?

Activity

Ask a person you support if you can look at their plan. Imagine you are their new support worker from another town or city and you don't know the person at all. Is there enough information in the plan? Is it detailed enough for you to support the person in the way they wish? Do they also have a more detailed support or care plan? Does it reflect their person centred plan?

Key points from this chapter

- Person centred approaches change the process of delivering a service to focus on how people want to receive it.

- To work effectively in a person centred way you need to be clear what person centred working is and what it is not.

What are person centred approaches?

Person centred approaches are:	Person centred approaches are not:
beginning with and from the person	observing from a distance
using creative ways of helping people with learning disabilities realise their aspirations, their hopes and their dreams	providing the same type of support year in, year out
making available the support the person needs to achieve the lifestyle they want	pushing individuals into the services that happen to be available, convenient or affordable
supporting better and more inclusive communities	always or necessarily about better services

References and where to go for more information

References

Falvey, M A, Forest, M, Pearpoint, J and Rosenberg, R (1997) *All My Life's a Circle: Using the tools: circles, MAPS and PATHS.* Toronto: Inclusion Press

Hunter, S and Ritchie, P (2007) *Co-production and Personalisation in Social Care: Changing relationships in the provision of social care.* London: Jessica Kingsley Publishers

Mount, B (1990) *Making Futures Happen: A manual for facilitators of personal futures planning.* Minnesota, MN: Governor's Council on Developmental Disabilities

Mount, B and O'Brien, C L (2002) *Building New Worlds.* Amenia, NY: Capacity Works

O'Brien, J (1987) A Guide to Personal Futures Planning, in *A Comprehensive Guide to the Activities Catalogue. An alternative curriculum for youths and adults with severe learning disabilities.* T G Bellamy and B Wilcox. Baltimore MD: Paul H Brookes

Pearpoint, J, O'Brien, J and Forest, M (1993) *PATH: A Workbook for Planning Positive Possible Futures.* Toronto: Inclusion Press

Pitts, J (2010) *BILD Guide: An introduction to personalisation.* Kidderminster: BILD

Sanderson, H (2000) *Person Centred Planning: Key features and approaches,* available at www.paradigm-uk.org

Smull, M and Harrison, S B (1992) *Supporting People with Severe Reputations in the Community.* Alexandria, VA: National Association of State Directors of Developmental Disabilities Services

Thompson, J, Kilbane, J and Sanderson, H (2008) *Person Centred Practice for Professionals.* Maidenhead: Open University Press

Wertheimer, A (ed.) (1995) *Circles of Support: Building inclusive communities.* Bristol: Circles Network

Legislation, policies and reports

All UK legislation can be downloaded from www.legislation.gov.uk

Policies and reports for Northern Ireland, Scotland and Wales can be found at www.northernireland.gov.uk www.scotland.gov.uk and www.wales.gov.uk respectively. Policies and reports for England can be found on the website of the relevant government department.

Human Rights Act 1998

Equality Act 2010

Department of Health (2001) *Valuing People: A new strategy for learning disability for the 21st century.* London: The Stationery Office

Department of Health (2009) *Valuing People Now: A new three-year strategy for people with learning disabilities.* London: Department of Health

Department of Health (2010) *A Vision for Adult Social Care: Capable communities and active citizens.* London: Department of Health

Department of Health and Social Services and Public Safety (2005) *Equal Lives: A review of policies and services for people with a learning disability in Northern Ireland,* available at www.dhsspsni.gov.uk

HM Government (2007) *Putting People First: A shared vision and commitment to the transformation of adult social care.* London: Department of Health

Putting People First (2011) *Think Local, Act Personal: Next steps for transforming adult social care.* London: SCIE

Scottish Executive (2000) *The Same as You? A review of services for people with learning disabilities,* available at www.scotland.gov.uk

Welsh Assembly Government (2007) *Statement on Policy and Practice for Adults with Learning Disabilities,* available at www.wales.gov.uk

Websites

There are short, easy read guides available for both the UN Declaration on Human Rights and the Human Rights Act, available at www.equalityhumanrights.com and www.justice.gov.uk

In Control (stories, factsheets and DVD clips all about personalisation) www.in-control.org.uk

The Dignity Challenge www.dignityincare.org.uk

Think Local, Act Personal www.thinklocalactpersonal.org.uk

Social Care Institute for Excellence (informative briefing papers and stories on social care TV about people with a learning disability and personal budgets) www.scie.org.uk

Chapter 2

Implementing person centred approaches when supporting people with a learning disability

Gary says, 'Charlie goes with me to the gym, to swimming, to the golf driving range. We go to football together. We love sport.'

Charlie says, 'When I started working with Gary he and his mum showed me his person centred plan. It says how important sport is to Gary. Lots of the work I do with him is helping him to stay healthy and enjoy sporting activities. I also support Gary to meet new people.'

Gary lives at home with his brother, mum and dad. Charlie is one of his personal assistants.

Introduction

Many people with learning disabilities need support so that they can have control of their own lives and take a full part in their community as equal citizens. Through experience we have discovered that our support will be most effective if the person is central to the whole process. This approach is often referred to as 'working in a person centred way' or 'having a person centred approach'. Making the person's support fit their dreams, interests and needs improves their life and it benefits the community in which they live.

Learning outcomes

This chapter will help you to:

- find out the history, preferences, wishes and needs of a person you support;

- apply person centred values in your day-to-day work taking into account the history, preferences, wishes and needs of the person;

- demonstrate ways to put person centred values into practice in complex or sensitive situations;

- adapt actions and approaches in response to an individual's changing needs or preferences including planning for future wellbeing and end of life care.

This chapter covers

- Common Induction Standards – Standard 7 – Person centred support: Learning Outcome 2

- Level 2 HSC 026 – Implement person centred approaches in health and social care: Learning Outcome 2

- Level 3 HSC 036 – Promote person centred approaches in health and social care: Learning Outcome 2

Finding out the history, preferences, wishes and needs of a person you support

If you are to put the person at the centre of the process of care and support, it is essential to find out about their history, preferences, wishes and needs. When you start supporting a person with a learning disability there is a lot to find out about them. Getting to know the person you support is an essential part of being a good support worker. It will enable you to work in a person centred way.

There are a number of ways to get to know someone and to gather information.

Talking to the person and observing them

The person is the obvious starting point. Lack of communication with words shouldn't stop you from learning from people. Through being with people in different situations, you can learn a lot about their likes and dislikes, what makes their life meaningful, and what they respond to. You need to continually listen to and observe the person you support in everyday situations. People may tell you things about themselves in words and by their actions. Someone may not tell you they dislike loud music but when you see them regularly putting their hands over their ears when the radio or CD player is put on too loud you have found out something about them by observation. We need to allow some people to tell us things in their own way through their actions, and we need to be skilled observers and have time to spend with them.

Talking to family members and friends

The next best sources of information are those who spend most time with the person, care about them and know them best – usually family members and friends, perhaps an advocate. You need to listen to and respect the information given to you by people who matter most to the person you are supporting. This is most likely to be their family and friends. They will know a lot about the person – their past, likes and dislikes and their dreams, and often they are willing to share this information with new support workers.

You need to listen to, and act on, information from family and friends.

Talking to other people who know the person

There might be other useful sources of information, such as the GP or practice nurse, if there are health issues involved. People in the local community, such as a local shopkeeper, community and religious leaders and neighbours may also be able to contribute in particular ways. If the person has a job, talk to their employer. If the person has taken college courses speak with their tutors. Sometimes former support workers keep in touch and can be valuable sources on a person's history. You should only approach these people for information with the permission of the person you support.

Talking to their advocate

If the person is able to speak up for themselves they may be able to advocate or represent their own views and wishes or they may need some support to do this. When working with people who are unable to speak for themselves, as well as being observant yourself you may want to work closely with their advocate if they have one. An advocate is independent and will be able to represent the views and wishes of the person. Advocacy is often a very good way for the person to present wishes and choices, express preferences and make informed decisions.

Care plans, health action plans and other records

There are a number of different plans and reports you can look at to find out more about the person you support, their history and support needs. Care plans and support plans are covered in Chapter 1 on page 14. In addition to the person's care or support plan, some people with a learning disability have a communication passport or a life story book or photograph album of family, friends, holidays etc. Sharing these with the person will help you to find out more about them.

When gathering background information on a person's history, preferences, wishes and needs, always remember to use appropriate methods of communication, e.g. gesture, sign or symbol systems and total communication, and share information with and about the person in positive and supportive ways.

Thinking point

Imagine that a new work colleague wants to find out more about you, but they only ask your boss and your mother what you are like. Do you think they would get a full picture, or would they only find out about certain parts of you? Your flat mate and friends in the pub might tell a different story.

Remember when you are gathering information on a person's history, preferences and needs all the people you speak to will have a different perspective on the person. Keep an open mind and use different people's information to build up a bigger picture.

What the person with a learning disability can tell you

You will need to gradually find out from the person you support what they want from life, their dreams for now and the future and what is important to them.

The areas of life a person might include in a plan will depend on their personal situations.

These are some life areas that might be covered in a person centred plan:

- How I communicate
- My hopes and dreams
- Where I live
- Who I live with
- Important people in my life
- My life story
- Things I used to do (and why I stopped)

- My good news – successes and achievements
- What I do in the day time
- Managing my money
- My possessions
- My social and leisure activities, including holidays
- My faith and beliefs

- How I look after myself and the support I need
- How I keep myself healthy
- Keeping safe both at home and in the community
- Food and nutrition
- Travel and mobility, including equipment, aids and adaptations
- How I can contribute and be part of the community

Apply person centred values in your day-to-day work

There are a number of ways that you can ensure that you are being person centred in the way you support people, and that you are taking into account their history, preferences and needs, including the following.

- **Use person centred values to inform your day-to-day work.** With any job it is easy to get into a rut and provide support today in the same way as you have for the last week, month or year. Sometimes we forget to question why we are doing things the way we are, it has just become 'the way we do things here'.

- **Regularly reflect on how you provide support** – thinking about the person centred values covered in Chapter 1 will help you. The book *Personal Development for Learning Disability Workers* in this series will help you to develop as a reflective worker.

- **Be person centred in how you write down information about how people want to be supported.** We need to write down information about the support people need to help us remember and to inform other people who support them. If it is written as if the person is saying it, this can help us to keep person centred. Always involve the person in putting it together.

  Make sure you check with the person if there is any information they want kept 'off limits' for more general use. For example, perhaps everyone might need to know about Katie's feeding and drinking support, but the support Katie needs for personal care is just kept to the female staff.

  If the person has communication difficulties and so hasn't said it themselves, don't make it seem that they have – write 'the team that supports Katie believe she no longer wants to go swimming because…'

  The plan should be clear about the specific level of support a person needs – too much and we will cause people to be frustrated or lose skills, and too little will leave them without having basic needs met.

Dionne is supported by three personal assistants in her own home. She and her family have put together a book containing photographs and information about Dionne, her likes and dislikes and how she prefers to be supported. When someone new comes to work with her she enjoys going through the book with them. It covers everything from her favourite soap operas and how she likes her hair done, to what her support needs are for feeding and bedtime.

- **Use the information to provide good support.** When you have found out more about the person you are supporting you need to put this information to good use so that you or others can provide high quality support. You should use the information to influence the type of support you provide so that you are focusing on their skills and achievements, not on what they can't do. You should begin to forge positive relationships with family and friends so that together you can help the person realise their dreams. As you develop in your role as a support worker you will learn more about the person and also develop better, more flexible ways of supporting them.

You do need to think carefully about what you do with the information you find out about a person. It is important that you remain open-minded when gathering information. Past history is important, but none of us want the people who know us now to judge us by the negative remarks someone made about us 20 years ago. You need to keep an open mind and not let past history restrict or influence your opinions of a person or the new opportunities you could offer them. Find out as much as you can, but remember:

- people change and grow;
- people sometimes get labelled, but the label may be out of date;
- the person may have had no opportunity in the past to represent their own interests and point of view.

Sometimes in our enthusiasm to do the right thing we can get carried away and forget that we are dealing with a real person's life. This means that there will be information that is private, sensitive and confidential. Imagine how you would feel if a group of friends wanted to discuss every aspect of your life – how much debt you have, what your relationships are really like, your bad habits – it doesn't bear thinking about!

Your work must therefore always make provision for privacy and confidentiality. Not everyone needs to have access to all information, nor should they have. The 'need to know' principle should apply. Sensitive and private information should be made available only to those who need to know and with the permission of the person concerned.

- **Use person centred thinking tools to help you.** These are simple tools that you can use with people with learning disabilities to find out more about them and to inform how you provide day-to-day support. Two useful tools are explained below.

1. **Sorting 'important to' and 'important for'**

   This person centred thinking tool helps to sort what is important to a person and for them, while working towards a good balance.

Important to / important for Adrian	
What is important **to** Adrian? *This is what makes him happy, content, fulfilled*	What is important **for** Adrian? *This is what needs to be in place for him to be supported, safe and healthy*
To buy his TV magazine every Tuesday	To have a regular chiropody appointment
Getting changed into smart clean clothes every time he goes out	To help him sort his laundry and put dirty clothes to be washed
Having lots of shirts and ties	Supporting him to eat his five portions of fruit and vegetables a day
Watching music programmes on TV	Make sure he locks the door properly
Going to the local pub on karaoke night	Encourage him to only take as much money as he needs to the pub and not all the cash he has
Calling his parents every Sunday	

   What do we need to do now?
   Use a calendar in his bedroom to put up appointments and favourite events.
   Spend some one to one time practising locking the door and checking it is locked.
   Help him find his favourite programmes in the TV guide.
   Try a range of fruit and vegetables he likes, find some simple recipes that use these and put them in a folder in the kitchen.

2. A one page profile or summary

These are the essential pieces of information about a person recorded on one piece of paper. It usually contains:

- the person's photo;
- what we like and admire about the person;
- what is important to the person;
- how the person wants to be supported.

This can be very useful to ensure that person centred support can continue in situations such as an emergency hospital visit, to help with the induction of new staff, or if there are relief staff working and people need to quickly know about the person.

For more information on person centred thinking tools go to www.helensandersonassociates.co.uk

Activity

Make a one page profile for yourself!

You can also find out more in the Department of Health guidance (2010) *Personalisation through Person-Centred Planning*. This joint good practice guidance published by the Putting People First and Valuing People Now teams has been developed to help local areas understand how person centred planning can help to deliver Putting People First. It is one of the commitments in *Valuing People Now*.

Being person centred in a complex or sensitive situation

In your day-to-day work supporting people you will sometimes be involved in complex or sensitive situations, such as when you go with someone to the doctor's, or support someone who is upset, or when you provide intimate personal care or talk to someone about confidential matters.

In these situations you will need to ensure that the person you are supporting is at the centre of what you do and that you do everything you can to understand and promote their needs and wishes. How you handle a complex or sensitive situation can have a long term effect on how the person feels and reacts and on their relationship with you, so you need to pay particular attention to your communication when working in a sensitive situation.

Knowing the person well and being person centred in your approach will help you to manage such a situation. The following table gives some examples of good practice in such situations.

Working in a sensitive situation

Good practice idea	Reason for working in this way
Listen carefully to what the person is telling you and reflect back what the person has told you.	It shows respect. Reflecting back the key points of the conversation can reassure the person you have correctly understood what they are telling you.
Think about where you talk to the person. It may be best to look for a quiet place where you will not be overheard.	Confidentiality and privacy are important. The person may feel more confident to talk to you if you are not being overheard.
Take your time and communicate in a way that is most suitable for the person. Adjust the words you use, your tone, the length of your sentences and the use of signs or symbols so that they are appropriate for the person and the matter you are discussing. Watch carefully for the person's responses, in both their verbal and non-verbal communication.	It shows you are working in a person-centred way and respecting the person's needs. Reflecting their vocabulary, pace and signs shows their communication pattern is acceptable.
If possible check with the person some while later to see whether they have understood everything or have thought of more points they want to discuss.	This gives an opportunity to check the understanding of the person involved as well as your own understanding. It also gives an opportunity to raise any other issues following a time for reflection.

Activity

Talk to your line manager about a recent complex or sensitive situation that you have been involved in with a person you support. Go through the four good practice ideas in the table above. Were you able to work in this way?

Adapting your support to an individual's changing needs or preferences

During our lives things are constantly changing and we have times of moving on, changes in our health and family situation. This is just the same for people with learning disabilities. We are all getting older, our preferences change, and our income may increase or decrease or our health improve or get worse, and new opportunities come along.

For people with learning disabilities these changes can have an impact on the support that they need, and their original person centred plan and support plan. So the approach to their support can go out of date, and you therefore need to review the person's support on a regular basis. This could be every year or every six months depending on personal circumstances, or more regularly if the person is having a time of major transition, such as:

- transition from school to adult services;
- leaving the family home to live in their own home;
- following a bereavement;
- if there are healthcare issues.

A review meeting needs to be held:

- when the person wants it;
- where the person wants it;
- with the people they want to come.

A review meeting can be like a person centred planning meeting. It will look at the original person centred plan and any additional supporting information, consider if there are any changes in the person's life, any external changes, such as when key staff may have moved on, a college course may have finished, or access to transport has changed. The review will also consider any achievements and goals fulfilled and any changes to the person's dreams and aspirations for the future. For example, perhaps the person didn't have the confidence to think about independent travel before, but now they would like to have the support to learn these skills.

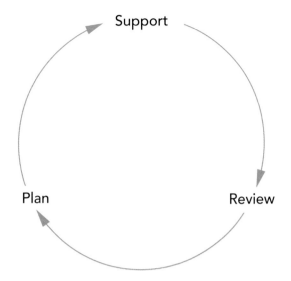

Planning for future wellbeing including end of life support

Planning with a person for their current and future wellbeing is a fundamental part of a person centred approach. In Chapter 6 you will learn more about contributing to an environment that promotes a person's wellbeing. When people come towards the end of their life there is often a need to take particular care to plan carefully for their ongoing support needs.

People with learning disabilities, their friends, families and carers need the same support and compassion as all of us do during times of change and loss. Traditionally, planning for the future and particularly for end of life care has not been very person centred. Often end of life care has been dominated by medical concerns at the expense of taking account of relationships and personal preferences.

An increasing number of people with learning disabilities are now living into old age and, by 2021, the number over the age of 50 is expected to increase by 53 per cent (Emerson and Hatton, 2008). This means that people with a learning disability are at increased risk of developing illnesses typically associated with ageing, such as cancer and dementia. People with a learning disability have poorer health than the general population.

Often, neither the person with a learning disability nor their carers are aware that they could plan for end-of-life care and support. Planning ahead for a person's needs towards the end of their life can be helpful not only for the person, but also for their family and the people who support them. It can often be a difficult and stressful time when people are ill, in addition to facing the physical symptoms of their condition, and seeing more medical professionals, they will have to face inevitable changes to their normal routine and the attitudes of people around them.

Recently Skills for Care and Skills for Health developed a set of core principles for social care workers supporting adults at the end of their life. The following seven principles underpin a number of core competences they have identified. You can use the principles below to think about how you would work with people with learning disabilities at the end of their life.

Principles for working with adults at the end of life

1. The choices and priorities of the individuals are at the centre of all end of life care planning and delivery.

2. Effective, straightforward, sensitive and open communication between individuals, families, friends and workers underpins all planning and activity. Communication reflects an understanding of the significance of each individual's beliefs and needs.

3. High quality end of life care is delivered through close multi-disciplinary and inter-agency working.

4. Individuals, their families and friends are well informed about the range of options and resources available to them to enable them to be involved in the planning, developing and evaluation of end of life care plans and services.

5. Care is delivered in a sensitive, person centred way that takes account of the wishes and priorities of the individual, their family and friends.

6. Care and support are available to and continue for anyone affected by the end of life, and death, of the individual.

7. Workers are supported to develop knowledge, skills and attitudes that enable them to initiate and deliver high quality end of life care.

Advance care planning is one way that people can identify their future wishes and care preferences. An advance care plan that has been developed with the person at the centre might include both health and social care providers. An advance care plan can set out the wishes of the person about how they want to be cared for now and in the future if their illness progresses or their condition deteriorates. This type of care plan can be particularly important if the person has communication difficulties and can't speak up for themselves.

More information can be found in Skills for Care (2009) *Common Core Competencies and Principles for Health and Social Care Workers Working with Adults at the End of Life*, available from www.skillsforcare.org.uk

These practical suggestions can help you to support a person to plan ahead for their future wellbeing including end of life care.

- Make sure that the person's capacity to consent has been assessed and then follow the appropriate legal framework for the country you work in.

- Use all possible communication methods such as repeating explanations, the use of pictures, or demonstration (e.g. showing someone a photo of the clinic before a visit) to help them understand what is happening.

- Make sure all medical staff introduce themselves each time they meet the person, always addressing the person directly, and clearly explaining their role and what they are going to do.

- Always listen to the person, and observe how they are behaving, informing the medical staff if it becomes apparent that their care or treatment could be delivered more appropriately.

- Tell the medical professionals about the person's life story and their likes and dislikes.

- Allow the person's existing routines to continue as much as possible and as they want.

- Support the person and their family in planning ahead for when they have palliative care, and for their final wishes.

Key points from this chapter

- The person is at the centre of the support you provide.

- Family members and friends are full partners.

- Your focus should be on the person's ability, what is important to the person and the support they need.

- In sensitive situations think carefully about your communication. Put the person at the centre, take your time, think about where you communicate and adjust your communication to suit their needs.

- Planning ahead for a person's needs towards the end of their life can help the person and also their family and the people who support them.

References and where to go for more information

References

Emerson, E and Hatton, C (2008) *People with Learning Disabilities in England.* Lancaster: Lancaster University, Centre for Disability Research (CeDR)

Falvey, M A, Forest, M, Pearpoint, J and Rosenberg, R (1997) *All My Life's a Circle: Using the tools: circles, MAPS and PATHS.* Toronto: Inclusion Press

Hollings, S, Tuffrey-Wijne, I, and Kopper, L (2009) *Am I going to Die?* Books Beyond Words. London: Royal College of Psychiatrists

Mencap (2007) *Death by Indifference.* London: Mencap

Mencap (2009) *End of Life Care: Best practice guide.* London: Mencap

Respond (2007) *People with Learning Disabilities: An ageing population,* available from www.respond.org.uk

Tuffrey-Wijne, I (2010) *Living with Learning Disabilities, Dying with Cancer: Thirteen personal stories.* London: Jessica Kingsley

Legislation, policies and reports

All UK legislation can be downloaded from www.legislation.gov.uk

Policies and reports for Northern Ireland, Scotland and Wales can be found at www.northernireland.gov.uk www.scotland.gov.uk and www.wales.gov.uk respectively. Policies and reports for England can be found on the website of the relevant government department.

Department of Health (2010) *Personalisation through Person-Centred Planning.* London: Department of Health

Skills for Care (2009) *Common Core Competencies and Principles for Health and Social Care Workers Working with Adults at the End of Life,* available from www.skillsforcare.org.uk

Websites

Helen Sanderson Associates www.helensandersonassociates.co.uk

The PMLD Network www.pmldnetwork.org

Understanding Individual Needs www.understandingindividualneeds.com

Chapter 3

Establishing consent when providing support

My support worker always asks me if I have any letters to read or if any bills have come, she asks if it's ok to read them as they are my private letters. She needs to read them so she can help me pay my bills, but she asks me first before she looks at them.

Frances has support to live independently

Introduction

This chapter is about the importance of getting the agreement or permission of the person you work with for the support you provide. Even when you are sure they are going to say yes, it shows respect when you ask first. Asking for and getting consent before you do anything is needed for all people, from people who need high levels of personal care through to people like Frances, who lives independently and needs support to pay her bills.

Learning outcomes

This chapter will help you to:

- explain the importance of establishing consent when providing care or support;
- analyse factors that influence the capacity of an individual to express consent;
- establish consent for an activity or action;
- explain what steps to take if consent cannot be readily established.

This chapter covers

- Level 2 HSC 026 – Implement person centred approaches in health and social care: Learning Outcome 3
- Level 3 HSC 036 – Promote person centred approaches in health and social care: Learning Outcome 3

The importance of establishing consent

Consent means informed agreement to an action or decision. The process of establishing consent will vary according to each person's ability to understand the information they are given and the implications of the decision they are making. It can also be understood as:

- being willing to do something such as take part in a research project;
- or to comply with treatment such as a medical procedure.

It is important you gain consent before a medical procedure.

If you were asked to consent to do something, such as take part in a shopping survey, first you would want to know more information, such as: Where will it take place? How long will it take? Will my responses be kept confidential? Do I get anything from taking part? Then you can give **informed consent.** If you found out that the survey took an hour and a half to complete and all you got was a free pen you might decide to say no!

Thinking point

How would you feel if you were finishing a report at work and the cleaner came into the office, didn't speak to you, but started dusting the desk, hoovering, and emptying the bin? What would your reaction be? While you understand the cleaner also has a job to do, think about how you would have liked them to approach the situation.

Asking for consent shows our respect

We show our respect for people when we ask for their consent when we provide everyday support. For example, if we are working with someone who has profound and multiple learning disabilities we ask if they are ready to go for a wash and change, and wait for some response before we take them, rather than just wheeling them off in the direction of the bathroom. Or if someone needs assistance with eating and we know they love tomato sauce on their fish fingers, we show them the sauce bottle and say 'would you like your sauce today?' and wait for their agreement, perhaps a big smile, rather than just dolloping the sauce on regardless. This helps people to feel their opinion matters and they are in control, and it supports people to develop communication skills.

> The Department of Health guidance on seeking consent says:
>
> if your work involves treating or caring for people (anything from helping people with dressing to carrying out major surgery), you need to make sure you have their consent to what you propose to do, if they are able to give it. This respect for people's rights to determine what happens to their own bodies is a fundamental part of good practice. It is also a legal requirement.
>
> *'Seeking Consent: working with people with learning disabilities' (Department of Health 2001) www.dh.gov.uk*

Ensuring people with learning disabilities fully understand all aspects of their support and can give voluntary consent whenever they have capacity, is an essential part of person centred support.

Factors that can influence an individual's capacity to consent

You should never assume that a person you support is not able to make their own decisions simply because they have a learning disability. Nor should you think that if someone once couldn't consent to one particular decision this means they won't be able to consent to a different decision in the future.

If you have doubts about whether a person has capacity to consent to a particular decision, then you, with other colleagues, will need to assess the capacity of the person. You should not do this on your own; you will need to work with others including family carers, colleagues and specialists such as a speech and language therapist or doctor. This assessment and the outcome should involve the person as much as possible and the process and the decision need to be recorded, including the details of who was involved.

Think about if family, friends or an advocate could help in the process of establishing consent. For example, they could:

- help the person understand the information about what is involved;
- suggest other ways of communicating information;
- help the person to understand the consequences;
- contribute to an assessment of capacity.

You might need to ensure that anyone supporting a person with making a decision is not influencing the person for or against consenting, even though they might have the person's best interests in mind. They might show this in an obvious way, for example clearly stating their opinion, or in a more subtle way through body language. A person with a learning disability could be highly influenced by a person they know well such as a parent or friend. For example:

- A parent may not want their adult son to go through a medical procedure as they want to protect them from any pain or discomfort.
- The brother of a person you support might not want his sister to start going out with a man she had met at the day service.

Surrinder's support worker was very confused that Surrinder was no longer enthusiastic about moving into his own flat, as he had earlier given enthusiastic consent to the move. He took Surrinder out for a coffee to talk it over and he found out that Antony, Surrinder's best friend in the residential home, was very upset that Surrinder was going to move away, and so he kept telling him not to move and to 'stay here with me'.

The support worker found out that Surrinder really did want to move but was feeling pressurised to stay in the home. The support worker helped Antony to understand that he and Surrinder could still go to the pub together, and have meals at each other's homes. The support worker worked with them both to prepare for the change. Surrinder was again able to consent to the move.

Other factors that can influence a person with a learning disability's capacity to consent include:

- Does the person have an impairment or disturbance of the functioning of their mind and brain? Is this temporary or does it fluctuate over time?
- Does the person understand the information regarding the decision?

- Can the person retain the information for long enough to make a decision?
- Does the person understand the implications of their decision?
- Can the individual communicate their decision to others?

Gaining consent for an activity or action

We must go through a checklist like this for each activity a person needs to consent to, because they might be able to tick all the boxes to consent to having their dental treatment but not to a major life decision such as consenting to getting married.

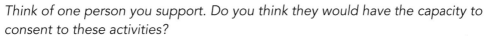

Activity

Think of one person you support. Do you think they would have the capacity to consent to these activities?

- *Having their hair cut.*
- *Having dental treatment.*
- *Going for a shower.*
- *Getting married.*
- *Moving into a flat of their own.*

To answer these questions and know if people can consent you need to be able to tick the following boxes:

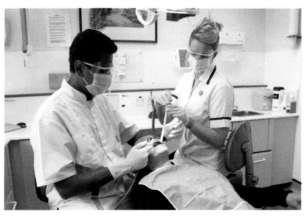

	✓
The person is competent and has the capacity to make the decision.	
The person has been given the right amount of information to be able to make the decision.	
The person understands the consequences of the decision, that is, what will or might happen.	
The person has given their consent voluntarily.	
The person understands what is involved including if there is any risk of harm.	

Discuss this activity with your line manager when you have finished it.

Tracey's doctor felt it was in her best interest to have a simple medical procedure. With the support of the staff who know her best they talked about it with Tracey, using simple words and a model of a human body. They explained she would have to have an anaesthetic and spend a night in hospital. She was told she would have to have a week at home after to rest and recover, and although she expressed disappointment at missing her weekly club, she nodded that she understood and agreed to this. The following day her staff asked her again why she needed the operation and how she felt about it, she responded with 'tummy better, yes! Sleep hospital no club' so they agreed that Tracey understood what would be involved and that Tracey could consent to this medical procedure.

Communication

See the *Communicating Effectively with People with a Learning Disability* book in this series for ideas on how to give information to people in a way that is meaningful to them and how to support them to communicate their decision to others.

Getting consent takes time

People with learning disabilities will need time and support to take on board information relating to a decision. We must not rush them, or insist on a quick decision. Many people with learning disabilities are compliant and they can be tempted to respond with what they think you want them to say rather than what they are really thinking and want. If you are asking if a person consents to a major decision, and you are worried they may say what they think you want to hear, you could consider asking another person who knows them well to ask them for their opinion or permission.

Privacy

Always discuss personal matters in a private place. It is important to always reassure the person that their personals details will only be shared with the people who need to know, for example, the doctor.

People are entitled to change their minds

People who give their consent for a specific activity are entitled to change their minds and withdraw their consent at any time, if they have the capacity to do this. On the other hand, people might decide to consent to an activity that they had previously refused. It is important to let people know this is their right and support workers must not show that they are annoyed or disapprove if people do this. Instead people should be congratulated for having the confidence to change their minds and show they are in control of their own lives.

However, if the person is withdrawing consent it is good to talk through with them why they changed their mind. Perhaps they were frightened or anxious, so they might need further reassurance and support before they can consent. It might be helpful for them to meet someone who has also gone through the same experience so they can reassure them, especially for medical or dental treatment.

How do we record consent?

It is not a legal requirement for someone to sign a form to show they consent. They can show they consent by telling you directly or in a non-verbal way such as holding out an arm for an injection. It is good to record who witnessed the consent, and how and where this happened.

Asma needed to have a filling in a tooth. The dentist explained what he needed to do – give an injection, drill and fill – and that it would take about 15 minutes. He told Asma he understood she was nervous, but that she wouldn't feel anything because of the injection, then he asked Asma if she agreed to have the filling. Asma leaned back in the chair and opened her mouth, showing she both understood and consented to the dental treatment.

Activity

Think about someone you know who doesn't have verbal communication. How do they give their consent?

Name	Activity	How consent is given/ communicated

Voluntary consent

Consent must be given voluntarily; the decision must be the person's own decisions and not influenced by others or out of a desire to please. Some people with learning disabilities are very compliant, especially to people they see as authority figures such as support workers or managers.

You must ensure that you don't manipulate, coerce, pressurise, instil fear in or blackmail a person into consenting to a decision or plan. For example, you must never suggest a bribe, a reward or a penalty to get someone with a learning disability to consent, even if you think the activity or treatment is in their best interests, such as having a tooth out. It would be wrong to say, for example, 'If you come to the dentists you can buy a DVD on the way home', or, 'Look no one else made a fuss when they had their injection, you don't want them to think you're a coward, do you', or, 'If you don't go to the doctors about that toe it could fall off!'

Steps to take if consent cannot be readily established

One way of establishing consent especially with people with complex needs is through a team agreement, where it is recorded with evidence of how and why a decision has been made. For example, Marvin has complex needs and cannot communicate his wishes verbally, but the workers who support him and his family need to review his activities as his physical health is deteriorating. Rather than the manager doing it alone, all the key people who know him best, including his parents, get together and record their decisions on a chart.

Situation to be reviewed	What are our facts and observations	What will we do instead	Name and date this was recorded
Marvin goes to the local swimming pool every week.	The changing rooms are too cold and he gets really cold and shivery afterwards. Last week he was cold for an hour and half after the session.	Marvin will stop using the public swimming pool. We will find an alternative place for him to swim and review this in two weeks.	

Gary, his current support worker, has a new job and will be moving on soon.	He always has a really big smile when Simon supports him.	Simon will become his key worker and there will be a handover from Gary starting next week.	
The sensory room have put up their prices and Marvin hasn't been for three out of four weeks because he has been too ill.	We agreed he smiles and is more verbal when we go to the shopping mall, and we can go when his health permits.	Marvin will stop going to the sensory room. For the next few weeks he will go to the shopping mall instead. We will review this in one month.	

The Mental Capacity Act

When people cannot give consent you need to refer to the Mental Capacity Act (2005) or the relevant capacity legislation for the country you work in.

The Mental Capacity Act (2005) applies to England and Wales; in Scotland you should refer to the Adults with Incapacity (Scotland) Act 2000; in Northern Ireland consent is currently dealt with under common law although there are plans to introduce capacity legislation.

Mental capacity simply means our ability to make decisions. These can range from everyday decisions about what we eat, to bigger decisions such as where we live and who we live with.

- Some people have limited capacity, e.g. can make simple but not straightforward decisions.

- Some people have fluctuating capacity, for example a person with mental health problems might not be able to make even simple decisions some days, such as what they want to eat, but on other days they are able to manage more complex decisions.

The Act came into force in 2007. Before this there was no legislation on mental capacity, other than common law and good practice. The Mental Capacity Act means now there is a consistent approach.

There are about two million people in UK who lack capacity to make decisions for themselves, which includes some people with:

- learning disabilities;
- dementia;
- mental health problems;
- stroke and brain injuries;
- people with temporary impairment or disturbance of the brain, e.g. people who are in a coma or unconscious or under the influence of drugs or alcohol.

The five principles

There are five principles that underpin the Mental Capacity Act 2005, and we have a legal obligation to ensure that every time we work with someone with a learning disability we work within the framework of these principles.

Principle 1	Assume a person has capacity unless proved otherwise.
Principle 2	Do not treat people as incapable of making a decision unless all practical steps have been tried to help them.
Principle 3	A person should not be treated as incapable of making a decision because their decision may seem unwise.
Principle 4	Always do things or take decisions for people without capacity in their best interests.
Principle 5	Before doing something to someone or making a decision on their behalf, consider whether the outcome could be achieved in a less restrictive way.

Assessment of capacity

The Act requires us to assess capacity on a decision by decision basis, rather than by making a single assessment of someone's capacity. There is a two stage test:

Stage 1 – the diagnostic approach

Does the person have an impairment or disturbance of the functioning of the mind or brain?

If yes, then the Mental Capacity Act (2005) can be used: move to the second part of the assessment.

Stage 2 – the decision making process

1. Does the person understand the information regarding the decision?

2. Can the individual retain the information long enough to make a decision?

3. Does the individual understand the implication of their decision?

4. Can the person communicate their decision to you?

Best interest decisions

The Act does not define what is meant by 'best interest' as this is different for each person. Instead it provides a best interest checklist.

1. The decision maker must consider whether it is likely that the person will at some time have the capacity and when that is likely to be.

2. The decision maker must involve the person who lacks capacity in the decision making process.

3. The decision maker must have regard for past and present wishes and feelings, especially written statements.

4. The decision maker must consult with others who are involved in the care of the person.

5. The decision maker must not make assumptions based on the person's age, appearance, condition or behaviour.

6. Where a decision relates to life-sustaining treatment the decision maker must not, in considering whether the treatment is in the best interests of the person concerned, be motivated by a desire to bring about his or her death.

For more information see *A Brief Guide to the Mental Capacity Act 2005*, by Elaine Hardie and Liz Brooks (2009).

Consent for use of personal stories and photos

In your role as a support worker you may need the people you support to give evidence or contribute to activities that are for the benefit of the organisation that supports them or to the staff who are employed there. This could be for a variety of activities. For example:

- Photos may be needed to go in an annual report or brochure.

- Videos or photos may be needed to go on a website.

- Staff may need to include a personal story for evidence for a qualification.

- An organisation may be doing a satisfaction survey and want some quotes from people who use it.

- A student may want to involve people in a research project.

- A member of staff may want to use someone's story as an example in a training session for new employees.

In all these cases we need to ensure people fully understand the implications of what is involved and we get their consent first.

David is the manager of a supported employment project and he needed to give a presentation to the council about how the project was going, to make sure they continued to fund it in the future, so he needed to show off all the good work they were doing. He asked all the people that the organisation supported who would like to be involved in his presentation and how. He didn't mention that it might have an implication on future funding as he knew this might put pressure on some people. He gave people several options, including not being involved, through to being interviewed and this being recorded to play in the presentation. Everyone then felt comfortable to say what they wanted; some just wanted to be videoed doing their job but not speaking, while others wanted to tell their story themselves. Everyone was given a copy of the final presentation to keep.

People need to be fully informed and know, for example:

- Who will own the photo?

- Can they choose which image is used?

- Who will see the publication when it is printed?

- Could the photo be used again and will they be informed?

Most organisations have a video and photo consent form. Ask your place of work if they have one and find out if it is a blanket form or one for individual occasional use.

Key points from this chapter

- Seeking a person's consent is an essential part of someone's support, regardless of their ability or disability. If you think someone doesn't have capacity there is legislation in England, Wales and Scotland to help you.

- Seeking consent is about helping the person to make their own, informed, choice, and different people will come to different decisions.
- Capacity means the person is
  - able to receive and retain the information;
  - able to trust the information;
  - able to use the information to make the decision;
  - able to communicate the decision.

References and where to go for more information

References

Department for Constitutional Affairs (2007) *Mental Capacity Act (2005) Code of Practice.* London: The Stationery Office

Department of Health (2001) *Seeking Consent: working with people with learning disabilities.* London: Department of Health

Hardie, E and Brooks L (2009) *A Brief Guide to the Mental Capacity Act 2005.* Kidderminster: BILD

The Scottish Government (2008) *Adults with Incapacity (Scotland) Act 2000: A short guide to the Act* www.scotland.gov.uk

Legislation, policies and reports

All UK legislation can be downloaded from www.legislation.gov.uk

Policies and reports for Northern Ireland, Scotland and Wales can be found at www.northernireland.gov.uk www.scotland.gov.uk and www.wales.gov.uk respectively. Policies and reports for England can be found on the website of the relevant government department.

Mental Capacity Act 2005 (applies to England and Wales)

Adults with Incapacity (Scotland) Act 2000

In Northern Ireland consent is currently dealt with under common law although there are plans to introduce capacity legislation.

Chapter 4

Encouraging active participation

> Kate was so used to having everything done for her that she was losing the skills she had learned. We encouraged her to put her own socks and shoes on with one-to-one verbal support. The smile on her face says everything as she concentrates hard to do this, we do her laces up just to finish the task and she gives a little giggle of self-satisfaction. Now she takes her socks and shoes off just to put them back on again!'
>
> *Clive – day opportunities coordinator for services for people with complex needs*

Introduction

This chapter looks at how we support people in a way that enables them to have maximum involvement in their support. That way people are empowered and become more independent and less reliant on others to do things for them. We call this active participation and it applies to support for all people with a learning disability whatever their abilities.

Learning outcomes

This chapter will help you to:

- describe how active participation benefits an individual;
- identify possible barriers to active participation;
- demonstrate ways to reduce the barriers and encourage active participation;
- describe different ways of applying active participation to meet individual needs;
- work with an individual and others to agree how active participation will be implemented;
- demonstrate how active participation can address the holistic needs of an individual;

- demonstrate ways to promote understanding and use of active participation.

This chapter covers

- Common Induction Standards – Standard 7 – Person centred support: Learning Outcome 4
- Level 2 HSC 026 – Implement person centred approaches in health and social care: Learning Outcome 4
- Level 3 HSC 036 – Promote person centred approaches in health and social care – Learning Outcome 4

What is active participation?

Active participation is a way of working that recognises an individual's right to participate in the activities and relationships of everyday life as independently as possible. The individual is regarded as an active partner in their own care or support, rather than as a passive recipient of care.

In the past the traditional model of services for people with a learning disabilities was to 'care' for people and staff were known as care workers or care assistants. This meant the general approach was to 'do things for people' especially for people who had higher support needs. So care workers would typically cook the tea and even make the drinks and people would sit in the lounge watching endless TV.

Encourage people to take part in everyday activities.

This differs very much from the current model of support for people with learning disabilities where the role of workers is to enable and support independence. Sometimes we refer to people being **actively engaged**; this means people are spending their time in an active and involved way rather than as an observer or having no fulfilling activities to do.

This chapter talks about how we can increase the participation of people in their everyday activities. We call this active participation, and it is a core part of person centred support.

Thinking point

Read these scenarios where people with learning disabilities are 'present' but not 'engaged' – that means they are not actively involved, rather they are just watching or doing nothing.

- *Think about why the support workers are acting in this way.*
- *What is the effect on the people they support?*
- *How does this make other people see the people with learning disabilities?*
1. *The worker is feeding someone who could feed themselves.*
2. *The support worker is looking up the cinema time on the internet in the office.*
3. *The personal assistant (PA) goes to the newsagent with the person they support and selects their usual magazine for them. The PA takes it to the counter and pays for it.*
4. *The support worker dusts and vacuums while the person with a learning disability watches TV.*
5. *The learning disability worker and person they support go to the supermarket. The worker holds the written shopping list and selects the items and puts them in the trolley that the person with a learning disability is pushing.*

What do you think should have happened if the worker was providing active support?

How active participation benefits an individual

When people are supported to actively participate in all aspects of their lives, then over time they will gain more skills, become more independent and need less staff support, and they increase in confidence and self esteem. Chapter 6 covers more on wellbeing.

People with learning disabilities need more than a person centred plan; they need support from people that enables them to achieve it. Active participation enables people to participate successfully in meaningful activities and relationships.

It enables us to look after ourselves and our daily needs

It promotes mental and physical health and personal development

The benefits of active support

It demonstrates our independence and autonomy

It helps us keep fit and mentally alert

It develops our talents and allows us to show what we can do

It gives us a sense of personal worth

It establishes common interests with other people

It allows us to express who we are

It provides the basis for friendships and living together

Taken from *Person Centred Active Support* (Mansell et al. 2005)

Possible barriers to active participation

Activity

Think about one person you support and two possible barriers they might experience to active participation. Discuss how you might overcome those barriers with your line manager.

There can be many barriers to people being actively involved in all areas of their life. The table below shows a list of barriers along with some of the reasons often given.

Barriers	Reasons
A person's contribution is not valued.	We need to value all the achievements people make, however small, and believe the extra time and trouble is worth it.
Service or individual workers' standards.	Some services may have high domestic standards that prevent people contributing. While it is important that washing up is done well for health and safety reasons, it doesn't matter if a table is laid incorrectly or a bed not made neatly. It is better that people have done these things themselves. Oddly chopped vegetables will taste just as good!
Manager's expectations.	Managers may want workers to see activities such as paperwork, or high standards of housework such as ironing the sheets, as being more important than investing time in active support.
Organisational restraints, e.g. time, staff available.	If there are insufficient staffing levels it is harder to implement active participation or the staff time available is not used effectively.
Existing timetables and routines.	If there are tight timetables allotted to certain activities this might prevent some people from being able to play their part.
Workers' roles and low expectations.	Some workers believe people's disabilities or behaviour prevents them from participating, and don't expect them to be able to increase skills given the opportunity.
Health and safety risks.	Overly strict health and safety policy and procedures may result in people having limited opportunities to engage to prevent them from possible harm, e.g. cutting up vegetables with a vegetable knife may not be allowed in case someone cuts themselves.
Workers' morale and motivation	Sometimes workers are not motivated to work differently, and have an 'it's easier to do it yourself' attitude.

● Staff in a particular team believe people with learning disabilities are dependent on them.	In some teams there is a culture that says it is their role to 'care' and so the workers prefer to do things for people. They may feel uncomfortable being paid to take a back seat role.
● A person's own domestic standards.	If a member of staff is a perfectionist, they may struggle to let people undertake some activities, or they may always want to finish off the task. This might be repeating the dusting which can make the person feel their contribution wasn't good enough.
● Complicated equipment.	Does the place where the person lives and works have appliances and equipment that are simple to use? Is this one of the main factors considered when choosing new appliances?
● Over-protection.	Sometimes support workers or parents can prevent active participation because of an over-protective attitude and a desire to keep the person safe.
● Lack of creativity.	Sometimes we need to be able to 'think outside the box' so we can involve people more. Hearing good news stories from other colleagues can help us transfer ideas into our work settings.

Reducing the barriers to active participation

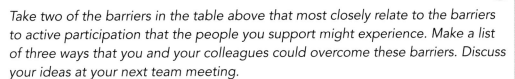

Activity

Take two of the barriers in the table above that most closely relate to the barriers to active participation that the people you support might experience. Make a list of three ways that you and your colleagues could overcome these barriers. Discuss your ideas at your next team meeting.

Making sure that there is clear communication in your organisation and with key partners, such as the person's family and friends about what each person can do, is a good way to make sure you don't over support people and stifle their independence. Also, working closely with colleagues in other services that support the person is essential so that a consistent approach to active participation is adopted. Make sure there is also a time to share and celebrate success together. (See the example about Daniel towards the end of the chapter, on page 61, as one example of how the levels of support he needs can be communicated.)

How to put active participation into practice

You can implement active participation for an activity with a person you support by following these steps:

- Break the task into small parts and let the person do whatever they can. For example, if you load the washing machine you can guide them to select the right programme and switch it on.

- Don't overwhelm the person with information while they are concentrating. Keep disturbances to a minimum, such as background noise or talking about an unrelated topic.

- Without being patronising, give the person praise and encouragement for their contribution and when they have learned a new skill.

- Be prepared to spend extra time, for example perhaps someone would have difficulty in watering the house plants because of mobility restrictions, but you could move the plants to a place where the person can reach them, and then return them to their normal place once they have been watered.

- Don't let setbacks prevent future involvement – we have all broken a plate or mug at some time when washing up! Perhaps it helped us learn not to stack the dishes too high next time. When we realise we make mistakes and learn from them it helps us remember that the people we support are learning too. It's OK to make mistakes.

When applying active participation be aware and take advantage of the person's strengths and talents as well as focusing on their support needs. For example:

- Where are their favourite places?

- Where are they most relaxed?

- Do they get bored easily?

- What are their concentration levels like?

- What music do they like best? When do they like to listen to it?

Think of someone you support and a household chore. Think of all the small tasks that make up that chore and write them in a list. Then think about how the person can be involved in each part of it.

For example if you chose washing up and the first job is to fill the bowl and add the washing up liquid – perhaps the person could squeeze in the liquid. If you need to do the washing up perhaps they could stand near you and pass the items to be washed to you.

For each item on your list for the chore you have identified think about how the person you support could be involved and add that to your list.

Talk to your line manager about the list you have made and how it might be implemented.

Some activities will naturally give a reward to people – for example:

- Some people might like using a machine so enjoy vacuuming.
- Going to the local live music club and buying drinks for friends at the bar is great for a folk music fan.
- A person who enjoys water might enjoy cleaning the bathroom.
- Eating a meal you have helped to prepare is always good!
- Making a drink for someone who thanks you.

Can you think of some natural rewards for a person you support and how you might use a natural reward to encourage someone to participate in an activity?

Applying active participation to meet individual needs

Even if someone has complex needs they can still actively participate in many daily living tasks rather than being a passive observer. For example, with support they could stir the cake mix, look through travel websites or brochures, eye point to which sweatshirt they want to wear. Remember every moment has potential for active participation. Your role is to enable people to 'be part of' and not 'done to'.

Trying things out little and often can overcome a history of failure and help people experience success. It doesn't matter if people's contribution is not for long or seen as not very much. Having the opportunity to be involved is all important.

Thinking point

Think of two people you support that have different support needs – how could they be actively engaged in planning a day trip to the sea, cooking tea, choosing what to wear, caring for a pet?

Using assistive technology

New technologies are providing different ways for people with disabilities to be more independent. For example, helping people:

- to be independent out in the community using mobile phones, GPS (global positioning system), panic alarms;
- to be able to communicate better – using a laptop, mobile phone, video phone or communication aid;
- to be more independent with their healthcare needs using medication dispensers, epilepsy sensors;
- to stay safe at home with alarm systems, door sensors.

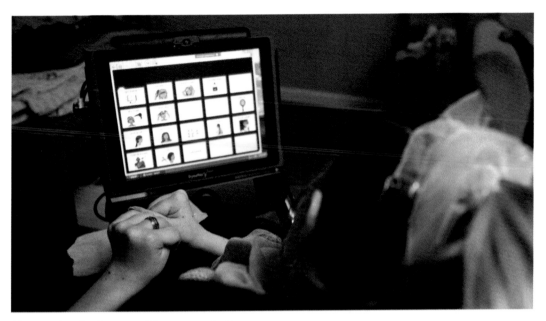
New technologies can aid communication.

Michael lives in his own flat and has a learning disability. He used to live with his parents and felt very frustrated as he wanted to live on his own and be able to invite his mates round and be more independent. He was able to move to a new flat installed with some gadgets that really make a difference. They are also known as personalised or assistive technology.

For example, Michael has a door sensor with a voice prompt which has a reminder set to prompt him to take his mobile and keys when he leaves for college. He also has a medication dispenser which reminds him when to take his tablets and he has also chosen a range of domestic appliances that have simple large buttons so he can do his own laundry and not have to rely on others.

You can see more examples of how people with a learning disability can use assistive technology on the HFT website at www.hftsmarthouse.org.uk

Agreeing on how active participation will be implemented

It is important that person centred approaches are shared between all people involved in the person's life, so that there is a consistent approach and the same support is given for the person in different settings. It is important to maintain confidentiality but to work in partnership and ensure the person is in full agreement about what is shared about them.

Using active participation to address the person's needs holistically

Active participation can help people gain more control over their lives, gain more independence and become more included as a valued member of society.

In John's old residential home he spent endless hours in front of the TV, meals were served and plates taken away, and every day was the same. He became increasingly bored, listless and depressed. He started to pick at his nails which then became a habit and he sometimes caused them to bleed. Now he is living in a new place where he is actively involved to the best of his abilities in all aspects of daily living – including taking out the bin bags on a Wednesday evening, delivering Christmas cards to neighbours, choosing the menu using photo cards, getting the washing out of the machine and going to the local pub. His favourite household chore is squirting on the shower cleaner.

He now:

- is more independent;
- feels more confident;
- lives a life more similar to his neighbours;
- has more skills;
- has less inappropriate behaviour;
- has better relationships with people;

and people say he looks ten years younger.

How to promote understanding and use of active participation

A plan like Daniel's example below can communicate to his team of personal assistants both his support needs and the contribution he can make.

I may want support to ...

 	**Get up in the morning** I have an alarm clock It goes off at 6.30 am If I am not up by 6.45 am please knock on my door and ask me if I am OK Tell me what time it is and remind me what I had planned to do today and ask me if I want to get up If I still don't want to get up please leave me for 15 minutes and come back and try again
 	**Have a wash** I like to have a shower every morning Usually I go straight to the bathroom when I wake up I can clean my teeth, but please put the toothpaste on the brush for me I can shower myself and shampoo my hair if you put the shampoo on for me and help me wash it all out Please help me to shave but I can put on my own deodorant and aftershave
	**Get dressed** I like to pick out what I will wear and can often get dressed by myself Sometimes I put things on back to front or inside out. If I do this, please tell me so that I know and can change it round I will let you know if I need any help to get dressed I will need help with my laces
	**Have breakfast** I can choose my own breakfast Usually I have tea and toast with marmite I can put the bread into the toaster and switch it on, but I need the staff to spread the butter and marmite I can wash up if you persuade me to! Do this by having a joke and making it fun. I like to pretend to say no at first!

Activity

Now you have read this chapter how would you describe your job as a support worker to a friend?

My role is to ....

...

You should now see that a key part of your job is to support the active participation of the people you support.

Key points from this chapter

- Reflect on your own practice. Are you enabling people to do as much for themselves as they can, and to take the lead wherever possible? Or do you sometimes do these tasks or make these decisions? Why?

- Expect people to increase the part of what they can do for themselves.

- It doesn't matter if people's contribution is not for long or seen as not very much. Having the opportunity to be involved is all important.

- To make active participation happen everyone including colleagues from other services needs to work together to deliver consistent support.

- Remember for people who have lived in services that have done most things for them, it might take time to get used to a different approach.

- Make sure all progress and achievements are praised and recorded if appropriate.

References and where to go for more information

References

Mansell, J, Brown, JB, Ashman, B and Ockenden, J (2005) *Person-centred Active Support*. Brighton: Pavilion Publishing

Websites

HFT Virtual Smart House (information about people with a learning disability using assistive technology) www.hftsmarthouse.org.uk

Chapter 5

Supporting a person's right to make choices

> Antonio used to go everywhere on a minibus or in a car, but he wanted to be more independent. He showed this by asking to walk to his local activities when the minibus was late! He now walks to his day service and the venue for his volunteering. Recently he has started walking to visit local friends too.
>
> *'I like walking – it's my choice and it's better for me too! I need to be careful; getting lost or getting hurt but I take care.'*

Introduction

This chapter is about being aware of people's right to make their own choices and ensuring they have the opportunity to do this in large and small decisions each and every day. In the past many people with learning disabilities were not given much choice, and support workers often took a lead in even very basic decisions. If you acknowledge your role is to support and enable you will recognise that people have the right to choose, and you have a daily role to create large and small opportunities for people to make choices and show their preferences.

Learning outcomes

This chapter will help you to:

- support an individual to make informed choices;
- understand why a worker's personal views should not influence an individual's choices;
- describe how to support an individual to question or challenge decisions concerning them that are made by others;

- use your own role to support the individual's right to make choices;

- use agreed risk assessment processes to support the right to make choices;

- manage risk in a way that maintains the person's right to make choices.

This chapter covers

- Common Induction Standards – Standard 7 – Person centred support: Learning Outcome 5

- Level 2 HSC 026 – Implement person centred approaches in health and social care: Learning Outcome 5

- Level 3 HSC 036 – Promote person centred approaches in health and social care: Learning Outcome 5

Support an individual to make informed choices

Thinking point

Think about when you support someone to do these activities; who takes the lead? Is it you or the person you support?

- *Who decides which way around the supermarket you go?*

- *Who decides which pub you go to?*

- *Who decides where you sit on the bus or in the cinema?*

Because many people with learning disabilities are reliant on others for support, this can mean their personal opportunities for choice and control are limited. This chapter will enable you to think about the right people have to make choices, even if they are highly dependent on others for care and support, and it will explore some practical ways to do this.

Where people do not have choice and control they can feel hopeless, oppressed, powerless and dependent. Empowerment is about having control and power in your own life. To do this, people need to feel confident and assertive and to know their rights. Advocacy is one way of empowering people with learning disabilities, but not the only way.

Empowerment is a dynamic process, not a static one. This means the level of support you give people needs to be flexible to how people's needs change. We need to be careful how we use the term 'empowerment' because it can sound as if 'we' the support workers are giving people with learning disabilities power.

Sometimes you will also have to help people to be realistic, and understand why in certain situations not all choices are possible. For example, if you were asked what holiday you would like you might choose to go on a month's Caribbean cruise, but due to the restrictions of money, and the amount of time off you can take from work, you might have to settle for a week in Blackpool instead.

Activity

Think about how you would enable one person you support to:

- *choose what they had to eat in a busy restaurant;*
- *choose what to wear in the morning;*
- *choose what to make for their evening meal.*

Discuss your ideas with your manager or someone who knows the person well. How you go about this will depend on the person's experience and their communication skills: for example, you might discuss what the person would like to eat in advance, offering them tangible choices (the real object, photos or pictures) so they can see and point to it. Make sure there is time to give the person the right information at the right time and in the right context.

Some people have had very limited experiences of making choices, so we need to remember it is a skill to be practised and developed like any other. Annie Lawton in her book *A Voice of Their Own* (2006) gives some suggestions of how we can help, which are shown below.

Ways of supporting people to make choices

- Teaching the mechanics of choice so people understand there are options and results, such as choosing between two activities or drinks.
- A good way to begin is to offer a known desired item and a neutral or non-preferred item.
- It can be easier to offer choices within activities, e.g. red or green paint in an art activity, rather than between activities at first, e.g. art or a walk in the park.
- Use real objects rather than representations unless you know the person can understand them, e.g. an apple and a pear rather than two pictures of fruit.
- If presenting a choice of two, swap them round to ensure the person isn't choosing the last thing you said or the one they look at last.
- Be aware of how your own bias might be communicated through your voice, body language or eye pointing.
- If people find choice hard don't offer an open question such as "which shop shall we go to first?" say "Smith's or Asda first?"
- Remember that asking people to make choices may be stressful for them.
- Get to know the person and find out how they usually communicate choices, perhaps smiles or grimaces, eye pointing or looking up, making an excited sound, trying to reach or grab.

A communication chart may help people to communicate their choices, especially for people whose actions communicate more clearly than their words. This short example shows how Tom communicates his choices at bedtime.

At this time	When this happens	We think it means	And we do this
Bedtime	Tom taps his mouth.	He is saying it is time to clean his teeth and go to bed.	Say, 'Yes, time for bed,' and support him to go to bed.

Learning logs

A learning or activity log can help us record information in a person centred way, that is with the person rather than about them. This records their choices and helps us support the person better in the future.

Here is an example of a learning log:

Date	Activity (what's happening)	Who was there?	What worked well – so continue	What didn't work well – so do it differently
....	Newtown Swimming Baths We went in the main pool as the small pool was closed for repairs.	Kelvin and two support workers – Jason and Ben.	Kelvin really enjoyed paying at the kiosk, and having a choice of hot chocolate from the machine afterwards.	The big pool was too noisy and cold, and Kelvin walked out of his depth and got frightened. Next time if the small pool is closed we will just have the hot chocolate then do an alternative activity.

You can find out more about learning logs and other person centred thinking tools from Helen Sanderson Associates at www.helensandersonassociates.co.uk

A learning log provides a way for support workers to record ongoing observations and what we have learned. The log focuses on what worked well and what didn't work well, and helps us to know what is important for the individual, what choices they have made and what preferences they have communicated. This information helps us to put people's choices into practice and provide better support in the future.

Activity

Complete a learning log for an activity that you do with a person you support. How can you use it to record choices?

The four plus one questions

This is another person centred thinking tool, developed by Helen Sanderson Associates. It gives a structured way for everyone to contribute, including the person themselves, and it helps to review what has happened so far and helps to plan the next steps or actions. This supports people's right to make choices and contribute to future activities and approaches to their care.

The 4 + 1 questions

Lucy has some health issues that are connected to her increasing weight, and are having a big impact on her quality of life. Her doctor says she must have a restricted diet and do more exercise or her health will deteriorate further. But Lucy doesn't like exercise and really enjoys her food! Her support staff have the challenge to help Lucy make some lifestyle changes that are her choice rather than having them imposed on her. They decide to offer her a range of new activities and record her response to them and use this information to decide on future activities. To do this they use a person centred thinking tool called the 4 plus 1 questions.

This is an example of a completed 4 plus 1 question sheet for Lucy.

1. WHAT HAVE WE TRIED?

We decided to see if Lucy would enjoy the aqua aerobics class to help get some exercise and meet other people, and take her mind off snacking at home in the evenings

2. WHAT HAVE WE LEARNED?

Lucy liked this activity very much as the pop music made her feel it was dancing and not exercising

3. WHAT ARE WE PLEASED ABOUT?

She took part and all the other members were really friendly

4. WHAT ARE WE CONCERNED ABOUT?

She will soon get fed up with this and won't want to do it anymore. Also there is a vending machine in the swimming pool lobby and Lucy made a big scene when she was discouraged from using it

When Lucy's support workers have answered the first 4 questions this will help them with the final + 1 question.

+1. SO WHAT DO WE DO NEXT?

Make sure support workers don't use the word exercise in connection with the class, but stress the dance and music part

Agree with Lucy before she goes out that she can choose to take a banana or an apple to eat afterwards, and not to take any money other than the entrance fee

Make sure all the staff and her friends praise her for going and encourage her in her weight loss

Remind her that when she has lost enough weight she can choose a new swim suit from the department store

Why your personal views should not influence an individual's choices

We all have our own values, beliefs and views based on our upbringing and our experiences. The personal views you have formed can impact on how you support people. You need to remember that everyone has different values and beliefs and as a support worker you must not let your values influence the choices that the people you support might make. You even need to be sensitive to how you talk about your views and values. It is important to say, 'This is what I believe or think, others have different views,' especially as people with learning disabilities can be compliant and they might want to please you rather than say what they want.

The General Social Care Council *Code of Practice for Social Care Workers* describes the standards of conduct and practice within which you should work. These are the standards that remind you not to let your own views influence the support you give. They say you must:

2.6 Declare issues that might create conflicts of interest and make sure that they do not influence your judgement or practice; and

3.8 Recognise and use responsibly the power that comes from your work with service users and carers.

You must not:

5.5 Discriminate unlawfully or unjustifiably against service users, carers or colleagues.

To find out more go to GSCC www.gscc.org.uk or The Care Council for Wales www.ccwales.org.uk or Scottish Social Services Council www.sssc.uk.com or the Northern Ireland Social Care Council at www.niscc.info

It is important therefore that you are fully aware of how your values and views may influence the way you support people and that you know about what to do to ensure you don't pressurise people.

The book *Personal Development for Learning Disability Workers* in this series contains more information on understanding how your values, attitudes and experiences can affect the support you provide.

Activity

Think about these three scenarios that show how the personal values of some learning disability workers have affected their support for people. What should have happened?

Katie is a vegan, she eats no meat, fish or dairy produce and when she supports people to go into town she refuses to go to McDonald's, even though they have requested this. Instead she takes people to the local vegetarian restaurant.

Bob is very concerned about global issues and so he insists they only have Fairtrade coffee in the house where he supports three people, and that they buy eco-friendly products and have the heating on very low, despite protests from the tenants and other staff.

Nazia supports an Asian woman who is going out with a young man she met at college. Nazia knows the family will strongly disapprove so she tells the young woman she supports that she must break off the relationship immediately or she will have to inform her parents.

Can you think of other personal values and beliefs that learning disability workers might have that influence how they support people? This might be because of their:

- *upbringing;*
- *religion;*
- *culture;*
- *politics.*

Supporting an individual to challenge decisions made by others

Thinking point

Think back to a time when someone made a decision that affected you that you didn't agree with. How did you feel? How did you feel about challenging the decision?

People with learning disabilities can also find that decisions are made by others about them and how they live their life that they don't agree with and they want to challenge. Challenging decisions made by other people, often people you might look up to or who have some authority in your life, can be a difficult thing to do. So you have an important role to play in supporting someone to challenge decisions they disagree with.

There are a number of practical things you can do when supporting a person to challenge or question a decision concerning them. For example:

- Listen carefully to their concerns and help them to be clear what they want challenge and why.

- Work with them to find out any additional information they may need. Remember information is power and people with learning disabilities are often excluded from information because of how it is presented and accessed. Lots of the information we get is presented in a way that means we have to be able to read, understand complicated words, use a computer, have the opportunity to speak to the right person, etc. You can help to overcome this by making sure information is in a form the person can understand. This could be as an easy read version or someone explaining it to them in meaningful bite-sized chunks.

- Support the person to understand the compliments and complaints policy of the organisation and how they can use it.

- Support them to know about their rights. Empowerment takes time, so this is a longer term activity you should be involved in.

- Help them to find other people who might be able to help, such as an independent advocate.

Using your role and authority to support a person's right to make choices

As well as other people making decisions that concern them without consultation, sometimes people with learning disabilities find their choices and opportunities restricted by other people's attitudes and beliefs. Think about what you would do in the situations in the activity below to support people to turn their personal choices into reality.

Activity

1. *Ranjit's family holds strict religious beliefs and they don't want their daughter to go to the disco, as there is a bar and she would not be home until after 11 pm. But all her friends at the day service go and she wants to as well.*

2. *Grant's elderly mother doesn't want her son to go on an activity holiday as she thinks he will catch a chill being outside, and is alarmed that canoeing is on the programme. He really wants to go.*

3. *Sarah has a chance to go for a week in Spain with friends from her social club. They are all going to save up and also do a car wash to raise the extra money. She is really excited as it's her first holiday abroad. When she tells the manager in the home where she lives he put a lots of pressure on her and says she must go on holiday with the other people she lives with, to a holiday camp in Somerset – all the others will be there so she must join in.*

Write down what you would do in each case. Talk through your ideas with your manager or an experienced colleague.

The practical actions that you can take to support a person with a learning disability to challenge the decisions of others that affect them or in working with them in making their choices a reality can include:

- Listening carefully to the person's choices and wishes and working with them to make them a reality.

- Supporting them to get any additional information they may need in a form they can easily understand.

- Working with them to explore different solutions and the advantages and disadvantages of various courses of action.

- Developing good partnerships with the key people in the person's life so that it is easy to raise concerns with them.

- Provide information on other sources of support, for example a local advocacy service.

Advocacy and people with learning disabilities

Advocacy is the process of speaking up on behalf of someone who is unable to do so for him or herself, regardless of your own opinion. It means presenting the interests of another from their perspective and ensuring that their wishes and feelings are taken into consideration before a decision is made. Advocacy therefore enables people to question or challenge decisions concerning them that are made by others.

Advocacy can be described as:

- representing the views and wishes of another person, or

- supporting a person to speak up for themselves to make informed choices, exercise their rights and have control over their own lives.

People who may need an advocate could be anyone who has difficulty in expressing their own views, especially in a formal setting, e.g. young people in care and people with mental health problems, not just people with learning disabilities.

For people with learning disabilities who use services, advocacy enables individuals and groups to make service providers aware of their views and interests. Advocacy is promoted in *Valuing People* (Department of Health 2001) and *Valuing People Now* (Department of Health 2009) and is seen as a major force for change in the lives of people with learning disabilities.

Advocacy has a lot to do with power. The advocate's role is to address the imbalance in power between service users and service providers. It is important for all people with learning disabilities to have access to an advocate, because it is often difficult for them to get what they want. They may not know what is possible, and may not know how to ask. It is especially important for people with learning disabilities who have communication difficulties, and who do not have much control over their own lives.

For more information the book *A Voice of their Own: A toolkit of ideas and information for non instructed advocacy* by Annie Lawton (2009) is very helpful.

Advocates are always independent. They are not connected to the carers or to the services which are involved in supporting the person. An advocate will work one-to-one with a person to develop their confidence wherever possible and will try to ensure that the person feels as empowered as possible to take control of their own life.

If you have a learning disability, an advocate will always:

- be on your side;
- listen to what you want;
- make sure people listen to you.

An advocate can work with people with learning disabilities to:

- speak out at meetings or to professionals;
- find information so people can make choices and sort out problems;
- change people's services if you want to;
- help people know about their rights and make sure they are respected;
- make difficult decisions;
- make a complaint if they are not happy about something.

Supporting a person's right to make choices and decisions

We tend to refer to **choices** as everyday choices, like what to wear, eat and do. We tend to use the word **decisions** when we refer to making significant and life changing choices such as moving to a new place, or having a different sort of support. Decisions can therefore be about changes in the future and so are outside of people's current experiences. They can be abstract ideas that are often hard to communicate. It is much harder to decide if you want to live in a new place you have never lived in, than decide whether you want fish fingers for tea, which is part of your experience and vocabulary. You still need to involve people in decision making as much as possible, whilst taking account of the laws on capacity in the country you live in, if you feel people cannot do this themselves.

The Mental Capacity Act (2005) (England and Wales), and the capacity legislation for the other UK countries, sets out a framework for people who may not be able to make their own decisions. You need to keep the law in mind when supporting people with choices and decisions. There is more about this in Chapter 3, on page 37.

How you can support people to make informed choices

There are a number of skills you can develop to support people with learning disabilities to make informed choices. The most important are communication and listening skills.

Communication challenges may include difficulties in using or understanding verbal communication, personality issues such as being shy or lacking confidence and a need for special equipment or skills such as signing. Below are some examples of how communication can help someone make informed choices.

People with learning disabilities are increasingly experiencing new opportunities to have roles where their voices are heard. Some examples are:

- They can join a self-advocacy group and speak up about issues with other people.
- They can have a role in evaluating the quality of services.
- They can be a trainer to other people with learning disabilities about their rights or train staff.

- They can contribute to research about people with learning disabilities.
- They can campaign about local issues such as college course closures.
- They can be part of policy making and service planning, for example through being part of learning disability partnership boards.
- If they have direct payments or individual budgets they can design their own services.
- They can be part of tenants' and residents' associations or other local groups that give an opportunity to make sure services are meeting their standards.

Complaints procedures

All organisations will have a complaints procedure to enable people who have a complaint to have it dealt with in an efficient and transparent way. Sometimes these might be written for staff or carers to make complaints, but we need to ensure people with learning disabilities can also use the procedure to complain.

Activity

Find a copy of your organisation's complaints procedure.
- *Find out if people with learning disabilities know about the procedure.*
- *Do they know how it works and who they complain to?*
- *Has it been used and what happened?*
- *Can you suggest any improvements so it is more accessible for people with learning disabilities to use?*

Six areas of good practice in relation to complaints and supporting people with complex needs to have a voice and communicate their choices:

1. Get to know people really well.
2. Improve communication skills.
3. Raise awareness of the human rights of people who have limited communication skills.
4. Improve access to advocacy.
5. Ensure everyone has their own complaints buddy – someone who will follow up a complaint on their behalf.
6. Have complaints procedures which also address complaints from people with complex needs.

Taken from *The Hearing from the Seldom Heard Project*, undertaken by BILD 2009.

Use agreed risk assessment processes to support the right to make choices

This story about Tom will help you understand how people can be supported to make choices and also to think about risk, using risk assessment procedures.

Tom wants to have a tattoo

He has been telling everyone this for the last three weeks, including the bus driver, all support staff, the local shop keeper and his brother. He wants a tattoo of a tiger like his favourite rock star. Martin, his support worker, went through the checklist with Tom so that he could be sure he was making an informed decision.

- What are the benefits?

- What are the risks?

- What is the experience of having a tattoo and the experience afterwards?

- What are the costs?

- What are the long-term implications?

- Are there any alternatives?

- What would happen if he doesn't have it?

Martin had no personal experience of having a tattoo so he arranged for Tom to meet one of his friends who had recently had one so he could hear about the experience first hand. He also:

- arranged a visit to a tattoo parlour to see what happened;

- checked out some suitable websites and then sat down with Tom at the computer so they could learn more together.

Tom was then able to weigh up if he really wanted to go through with having his tiger tattoo… and he decided not to. A couple of months later Martin asked Tom how he was feeling about the decision he had made and he said he was pleased he decided not to.

Martin made sure he did everything possible to enable Tom to make his own decision, and understand the consequences if he had gone ahead with the tattoo. This meant Tom felt he had made the decision and not allowed others to make it for him.

You can adapt these questions to use with other people who need to make a big decision.

1. What might be the positive effects of being able to make choices? What might be the negative effects if choice and control are denied?

2. In what way can you enable a person with a learning disability to make their own choices? For example, providing information and supporting new experiences.

Managing risk to maintain the right to make choices

You must balance your duty of care to protect the people you support with opportunities to choose what they want, even when their choice may have an element of risk. We need to assess and manage the risk their choices present, and give a full explanation if people's choices cannot be followed or if the risks are considered to be too high. You must remember to include the person in their risk assessment as much as is possible. See Chapter 7 on risk for more information.

The book *Duty of Care for Learning Disability Workers* in this series covers more on managing the tensions between duty of care and upholding the person's rights.

Key points from this chapter

- 'The most powerful and the most convincing advocates for change are people with learning disabilities themselves' (Mittler 1996).

- Choice is about:
    - preference – things you like to do;
    - opportunity – to do those things;
    - control – of when, where and with whom those opportunities will occur.

- Your role is to always ensure that the people you support have the right to make both small choices and major decisions that affect their lives.

- You must also ensure that others understand and listen to what people with a learning disability are saying.

References and where to go for more information

References

Lawton, A (2006) *A Voice of Their Own.* Kidderminster: BILD

Mittler, P (1996) Advocates and Advocacy, in *Changing Policy and Practice for People with Learning Disabilities.* P. Mittler and V. Sinason. London: Cassell

Walmsley, J and Downer, J (1997) Shouting the Loudest: Self Advocacy, Power and Diversity, in *Empowerment in Everyday Life: Learning Disability.* P Ramcharan, G Roberts, G Grant and J Borland. London: Jessica Kingsley

Ward, L (1998) *Innovations in Advocacy and Empowerment for People with Intellectual Disabilities.* Chorley: Lisieux Hall

Legislation, policies and reports

All UK legislation can be downloaded from www.legislation.gov.uk

Policies and reports for Northern Ireland, Scotland and Wales can be found at www.northernireland.gov.uk www.scotland.gov.uk and www.wales.gov.uk respectively. Policies and reports for England can be found on the website of the relevant government department.

Codes of practice for social care workers are available from:

Care Council for Wales www.ccwales.org.uk

General Social Care Council (England) www.gscc.org.uk

Northern Ireland Social Care Council www.niscc.info

Scottish Social Services Council www.sssc.uk.com

Websites

Hearing from the Seldom Heard materials are downloadable from www.bild.org.uk

Person centred thinking tools from Helen Sanderson Associates are downloadable from www.helensandersonassociates.co.uk/

Chapter 6

Promoting a person's wellbeing

> I go to church with my sister, I pray and sing and ask God to help my dad get better. Being a member of the church is good; people are friendly and help us.
>
> *Rajinder is from a Sikh family, but she and her sister are Catholics. Her faith and being a member of a local church are important to her.*

Introduction

We now recognise that in addition to supporting people with personal care and independent living skills, it is really important to support their wellbeing which is essential to living a fulfilled, happy and healthy life. Wellbeing covers many aspects of our life such as identity, self-esteem and spirituality. In this chapter we explore what the support worker can do to promote the wellbeing of the people they support.

Learning outcomes

This chapter will help you to:

- explain how individual identity and self-esteem are linked with wellbeing;
- describe attitudes and approaches that are likely to promote an individual's spiritual and emotional wellbeing;
- support an individual in a way that promotes a sense of identity and self-esteem;
- demonstrate ways to contribute to an environment that promotes wellbeing;
- explain the links between identity, self-image and self-esteem;
- analyse factors that contribute to the wellbeing of individuals.

What is wellbeing?

Wellbeing is a term that has gained in popularity in recent years, and it relates to our emotional, psychological and spiritual state of being. It is a broad term that is about 'being well in ourselves' or 'being in a good place'. We might use words like happy, relaxed, positive, confident, assured, peaceful, healthy and fulfilled as coming under the umbrella of wellbeing.

In the past services focused on the physical care, support and behaviour needs of people with learning disabilities. Some professionals even believed people with learning disabilities didn't experience emotions to the same extent as non-disabled people and thought they weren't capable of making close relationships with others. So, for example, this led to people not being given opportunities to grieve following bereavement or given support and treatment for depression. Now we understand people with learning disabilities experience the full range of emotions as we all do and we recognise support as much more of a holistic activity that takes into account all areas of a person's life.

Wellbeing includes many dimensions of our lives such as our spirituality and religious beliefs, our emotions, our sexuality, how we experience our culture, our social class and status, and our political views. Our wellbeing improves when we have positive experiences, relationships and roles.

In your role as a support worker you need to support people in all areas of their lives, including promoting their wellbeing. This might involve creating opportunities for the people you support to develop friendships and personal relationships, being included in their local community, having opportunities to explore their spirituality and sexuality and having roles which give them status. We will talk about these later on in this chapter.

A person's wellbeing may be helped by:

- a sense of hope;
- good self-esteem (feeling good about yourself);
- an ability to communicate your wants and needs;
- an ability to make and develop relationships with other people including acquaintances, friendships, family ties and close intimate relationships;
- an ability to show warmth and affection;
- experiencing pleasure or enjoyment;
- making your own choices and decisions and having control over your life;
- becoming more self-confident;
- having a sense of achievement;
- becoming more independent;
- coping with stresses and problems;
- being praised for achieving;
- having someone to share important things with;
- knowing you are valued and important;
- feeling included;
- feeling safe and secure.

Thinking point

Pick two of the points on the list above. How have you promoted these aspects of wellbeing for a person with a learning disability that you support?

How individual identity and self-esteem are linked with wellbeing

It is our identity which makes us unique. If you are asked, 'Who are you?', you would probably use some of the following to define yourself.

Some of the factors that make up our unique identity

- Name
- Age
- Where you live
- Where you were born and brought up
- Educational background
- Occupation
- Marital status
- Whether you have children
- Family background
- Family relationships
- Self-image
- Friendships past and present
- Past experiences
- Religious beliefs
- Core values
- Likes and dislikes
- Hobbies
- Dreams and aspirations

Your identity is formed through your interactions with others, but you also actively take part in forming your own identity. Our identity gives us our status in our community; it combines 'how I see myself' and 'how others see me'.

Identity is about recognising that each person is a unique individual, and is about being aware of our similarities to, and differences from, other people. We need to have a level of self awareness to know our identity or who we are, and we use this to be able to form and maintain relationships with others.

We don't want to minimise people's impairments and their need for support, but a person with a learning disability has a much bigger identity than their label of learning disability, just as your identity is far more than your role as a support worker. It is essential that people with learning disabilities are not defined only by their label of learning disability but by their wider identity. For example they may be a cricket fan, an aunt, a darts player, a sister, a 'good laugh', etc.

Activity

We all have lots of identities and social roles. Think of both a person you support and yourself, and make a list of all the other labels, roles and relationships that can describe you and give you both your unique identity, for example:

Me	Someone I support
Jamaican	Brother
Mother	Chelsea fan
Sister	Good sense of humour
Good cook	Easy going
Good listener	Great darts player

Many people with learning disabilities have had only minimal or limited opportunities to explore some aspects of life and they have also few opportunities to be able to convey this information about themselves to others. Other people have had lots of opportunities, and can communicate about all they have done and are going to do. How will this affect their wellbeing?

Historical issues about the identity of people with learning disabilities

In the past, professionals gave people a set of labels, usually after following an assessment and using rating scales, and this is how they were known. These labels would be very offensive to us today, for example, someone we know as a brother, a West Bromwich Albion fan, a TV soap addict and as having a learning disability, in the past may have been labelled as 'low grade', an 'imbecile' or 'retarded'. These labels focused on what people could not do and grouped them with others who had similar abilities, denying their individual personality and identity. The result was to 'pigeonhole' people into groups with labels.

This is why today the self-advocacy movement has a slogan 'label jars … not people!'

People were denied an individual identity apart from the learning disability label placed on them by non-disabled others. In some institutional settings such as hospitals, people were not allowed to keep many personal possessions, or there was nowhere to keep them safe. In some places

everyone had to wear the same type of clothes and they were given the same haircuts so there was no opportunity for self expression. This is still the experience of many people with a learning disability today in other countries around the world.

Only in recent times has the emphasis shifted so that we now see the person first and not their impairment. As a learning disability worker your role is to see people as having their own identity and celebrating their diversity.

How do people with learning disabilities relate to having a learning disability, and how does this affect their identity?

People with learning disabilities are increasingly aware of and openly acknowledge their identity as a person with learning difficulties or learning disability. Many people actual prefer the term learning difficulties, especially those who join self advocacy groups. In the past it was almost a taboo to refer to 'learning disability' in front of people, but now this has changed with the awareness of the social model of disability, where we see that the barriers to being fully included are with the world the person lives in, rather than with themselves. Having a learning disability is now seen as another difference to celebrate, as we do with people from other ethnic, disability and community groups.

Jan Walmsley, a researcher and writer, wrote that, 'self-advocacy can be seen as a way of celebrating difference rather than denying it, and opens the way for a recognition of people with learning difficulties as a group with an identity of its own, an identity to own publicly, not hide'.

Walmsley and Downer, 1997

As support workers, we need to show respect for and value the differences between all people.

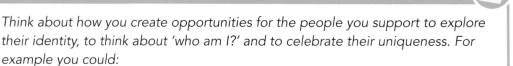

Activity

Think about how you create opportunities for the people you support to explore their identity, to think about 'who am I?' and to celebrate their uniqueness. For example you could:

- *help to make a scrap book of special events;*
- *make a family tree;*
- *put together a photograph album of their life so far or their wider family;*
- *make a PowerPoint presentation or interactive DVD entitled 'This is me';*
- *help them to write their life story;*
- *make a collection of items that relate to their faith or culture;*
- *make a collection of postcards of all the places they have visited.*

All these activities are valuable because they will help the person to explore their identity and give them a sense of achievement. The activities will also create something that they can show others to share and explain who they are. As people develop their sense of identity they will increase their sense of wellbeing.

If we have positive self-esteem we project this to other people. Other people relate to us according to how they find us, so if we are confident and happy people will treat us very differently than if we come across as having low self-esteem.

Attitudes and approaches for promoting wellbeing

You need to describe the people you support to others in a positive way and relate to their unique personalities rather than define them by their labels – remember they are people first.

One of the person centred tools is called 'like and admire', and it is suggested that this description goes first into the person's notes and records. It is designed so that any workers who support the person can get to know them first as a unique individual rather than seeing a label or a syndrome first, or even what support they need. This sheet says what we like and admire about a person. This is Mo's 'like and admire':

Mo is full of fun; he has a great smile and brightens up everyone's day with his singing. He loves a mug of hot chocolate (but he has to have squirty cream that he piles on). He is an EastEnders fan and enjoys a game of snap! (but can be known to cheat). He loves to go out in the car and knows how to disappear fast when it's time to wash up.

We need to recognise that each person is a unique individual who needs a unique approach to meet their needs, preferences, hopes and dreams. To get Mo to do his fair share of washing up, his support workers make a game of it, teasing him so that after lots of laughs and delays Mo finally grabs the tea towel. Fun and games are how he communicates and builds relationships, and this ritual is an important part of his life. This approach, however, would be completely unsuitable for another person.

For more information on person centred thinking tools go to the Helen Sanderson Associates website at www.helensandersonassociates.co.uk

Promoting a sense of identity and self esteem

We all need opportunities to have peace and relaxation, fun and excitement, to be stretched, step out of our comfort zone, times of privacy, times of celebration, time to grieve, etc.

Activity

Think about how many times in the last month you had any of the opportunities listed above. How did they affect your wellbeing?

Now think about how often someone you know with learning disabilities had these opportunities in the last month. Are the two answers different? If so why do you think this is?

Holistic support for people with learning disabilities which promotes their wellbeing should include opportunities:

- to belong;
- to develop significant relationships including intimate relationships;
- to contribute to others;
- to grow, develop and achieve;
- to relax;
- to enjoy and have fun and celebrate;
- to be an equal citizen.

These are explored in more detail below.

Opportunities to belong

We all need to have a sense of belonging. An essential part of person centred support includes how the person can strengthen their connections with their community, including opportunities to contribute as well as to take part.

Communities can be:

- geographical areas – such as our street, neighbourhood, our town;
- communities of interest – with people who share our passions and interests, whether for a sports team, rock band or a pastime such as camping or gardening.

Community can be understood as the set of ties and connections that a person has with others. When people are asked what makes them feel part of their community they usually respond with words and phrases such as:

- friends;
- a sense of belonging;
- similar interests;
- shared beliefs and goals;
- common experiences;
- knowing people;
- feeling valued;
- making a contribution.

Most of us belong to several different communities, and we should ensure that our person centred support actively develops opportunities for people to be part of their chosen communities too. This will facilitate new friendships, interests and opportunities for personal growth and fulfilment.

Activity

1. *Make a list of the groups you are a member of.*
2. *Now do the same for a person with a learning disability that you know well.*
3. *How do the two lists compare?*
4. *What are the wider groups you might both be members of, e.g.:*
   - *family;*
   - *clubs;*
   - *workplace;*
   - *church;*
   - *town/community;*
   - *nationality.*
5. *What are the differences? Talk to one of your colleagues about why this is.*

The different community roles in the table below might help you think more about the communities that the people you support belong to.

● Clients	When we use a service that helps us, e.g. the hairdresser or the Citizens Advice Bureau.
● Customer	When we use a service to buy things, e.g. the bank, shops, post office.
● Citizens	When we vote, complain, campaign.
● Service user	When we use specialist services, e.g. a day service for people with learning disabilities.
● Patient	When we use a health service, such as the doctor, dentist or physiotherapist.
● Employee	When we have a paid job.
● Member	When we join a club, society, church or gym.
● Passenger	When we travel on a bus or train.
● Participant	When we take part in surveys and other activities.
● Volunteer	When we help out in projects but don't get paid, e.g. gardening or working in a charity shop.
● Student	When we take part in learning.
● Supporter	When we support a sports club, such as Chelsea or the local team.

Supporting a person to connect with their community

You may find some or all of the following suggestions helpful when thinking about your role in supporting a person to connect with their community.

- Does the support or person centred plan identify what the person does with others in the community and how they share their gifts and interests?
- Does it make connections with people and places, their family and the network around the person?

- Does the support or person centred plan identify local resources where the person's gifts might be welcome, such as local sports clubs, neighbours, workplaces, shops, pubs, church, temple or mosque, and community groups?

- Do participants in the support or person centred plan open up their own resources, contributions and networks to the person?

- Does the person have the opportunity to share activities and interests with like-minded people?

- Are you using small successes to build greater confidence?

- Are you thinking about what works and what doesn't work to make ongoing improvements or try different approaches?

- Have you thought about how the person can move from just using community facilities to contributing by having an active role?

Opportunities to develop significant relationships

Imagine for just one moment having no friends or family! Most would say these are the most precious things we have, yet for people with learning disabilities often their circumstances have limited their opportunities to develop or maintain meaningful relationships. It is part of your role as a support worker to help people to build and keep friendships and relationships with family, as without this people's wellbeing will be severely affected.

Opportunities to contribute to others

We all, including people with learning disabilities, need to be interdependent on others, and this helps to give us positive status and identity. We feel good when we help and show kindness to other people. Simple things can mean a lot, for example:

- sending a card to someone to say get well or thank you;

- helping at a community event such as being a marshal at a fun run;

- feeding a neighbour's pet;

- telling a friend or neighbour when you are going shopping and asking if they want anything brought back.

People who have the time, skills and commitment might like to take up volunteering or join the local Timebank.

Does your support to people with learning disabilities enable them to give to others and contribute to their community and so increase their self-esteem?

Opportunities to grow, develop and achieve

We all need opportunities in our life to grow and develop, to learn new skills and experience new things. Without new experiences life can get very boring and monotonous.

Taking advantage of community opportunities or helping people to stay in touch with their family and friends are important in identifying new experiences. Equally you can introduce the person to new experiences through day-to-day activities, for example by cooking a new meal for dinner, listening to new types of music on the radio or walking home by a different route to see the canal or the spring flowers.

Opportunities to relax

It's not good for us to always be on the go. Do you think the person you support gets enough time to relax and have some 'down time'? Also it is good for people's wellbeing to have some private time in their own room, if this is their choice.

Pauline gets very 'wound up' and stressed with a lot of noise and activity in the house, so Martha, her support worker, made her an appointment for an aromatherapy massage. Pauline really enjoyed this and staff noticed when she came home she was much calmer and more content, so she now has one on a fortnightly basis.

Opportunities to enjoy and have fun and celebrate

The people with learning disabilities you support need to have opportunities to feel good about themselves, share their success and achievements and be part of celebrations.

Activity

Think of a recent time when you last felt good about yourself or you were 'walking on air'. Perhaps you:
- *passed an exam or your driving test;*
- *you had a night out with friends;*
- *you got a new job or promotion;*
- *you had an invitation to a party or wedding.*

How could you enable more opportunities like this for the people you support?

Opportunities to be an active citizen

Tom was very concerned about a large tree outside his flat. It had low branches that stuck out into the pavement, and it dropped lots of leaves that could make the pavement slippy when it had rained. He was also worried the tree would get blown down one windy night. Sometimes it seemed that worrying about the tree was stopping Tom enjoying other activities as he was always talking about it, at mealtimes, when they went shopping and to the pub. It was also getting a bit tiresome for Tom's flat mate and his support workers.

Ruth, one of his support workers, knew this was an important issue to Tom, and decided to be proactive. She helped him take a photo of the tree. She then wrote a letter on Tom's behalf about his concerns, which he then signed. She supported Tom to post it to the relevant part of the council. Tom was delighted to get an official letter back, asking him to meet the officer responsible for trees outside his house one morning. The council officer listened to his concerns and he reassured Tom it was safe and natural for a tree to bend in high winds, but he agreed some maintenance work was needed on the lower branches. This experience helped Tom to be less anxious, to feel that he was listened to, and to have a sense of pride that he had helped make his neighbourhood a safer place.

What could you do to support people to be an active citizen?

- Do you support people to be on the electoral register and vote at the elections?

- Do you support them to know what is happening in their area and to complain or bring matters to the council's attention, such as anti-social behaviour?

- Do you encourage people to understand the value of recycling and to put this into practice?

- Do you support people to watch the news on TV and understand some of the issues?

Ten top tips on feeling good from *All About Feeling Down*, a book written for people with learning disabilities aged 14 to 25 (Foundation for People with Learning Disabilities 2003):

1. Keep in touch with family and friends.
2. Talk to friends about your worries or problems.

3. Do activities you enjoy.

4. Look after your health.

5. Take time to relax.

6. Find interesting and positive ways to spend your days.

7. Have regular exercise.

8. Speak up for yourself.

9. Let your feelings out – don't bottle them up.

10. Get in touch with your feelings.

Contribute to an environment that promotes wellbeing

You need to think about promoting wellbeing in the day-to-day support of people in the community. Over the past few decades there has been a significant change in services for people with learning disabilities, and in our attitudes and awareness. In the past we believed people with learning disabilities had to be 'cared for' by 'professional experts' and 'care workers'. Now we understand that people with learning disabilities need support to live ordinary lives and be active citizens.

This means you should be proactive in enabling people with learning disabilities to be part of their local communities and to develop meaningful relationships with people who are not just there to support them in a paid capacity. Your role as a support worker is to facilitate people being part of other social groups, so they can have the opportunity to develop interests and skills and to make new connections and acquaintances which may lead to friendships.

Life experiences which affect our wellbeing

The life experiences listed below can affect all of us at different times in our lives. We need to ensure that if the people with learning disabilities we support also face these difficult life experiences they are given the personal support they might need. For example, we might experience:

- poor physical health;

- times of change and transition with where we live or our jobs;

- bereavement;

- social isolation – having few significant friendships;

- abuse, bullying and harassment;

- being let down by a friend, colleague and for people with learning disabilities the staff who support them;

- not being listened to;

- having limited social roles;

- poverty and debt;

- break-up or loss of a significant relationship and for people with learning disabilities this can include the staff who support them.

These experiences can be made more difficult if people with learning disabilities have difficulty in interpreting and communicating emotions. Your role is to create an environment that supports people when they have difficult life experiences.

Report writing

We can learn a lot about people's personality and behaviour by reading written descriptions about them. For people with learning disabilities much of what is written about them, which affects how they are treated, refers to their disability and ignores other parts of their identity, such as gender, ethnicity, religion, sexual orientation, etc. Labelling can lead to an erosion of identity and restricts people's ability to make choices. Written descriptions can often be negative, unhelpful and even frightening, and lead to staff having low expectations, so we need to make sure we write in a positive way about the person. For example, we can describe behaviour as being challenging and not the person themselves!

> Instead of writing:
>
> Simon is grumpy and in a bad mood in the mornings and is often irritable to the staff. If you hurry him he will swear and shout at you. Once he threw a slipper at a student!
>
> You could put:
>
> Simon likes a quiet and slow start in the morning. First just open his curtains or put on the bedside light in the winter and put on the radio, and leave him for 10 minutes. Then take him a cup of tea, and politely suggest he sits up. Don't be directive or 'tell him'. Give him another 10 minutes, and then encourage him to get out of bed, and remind him breakfast will be put out when he comes downstairs.

Analyse factors that contribute to the wellbeing of individuals

Wellbeing is a complex idea and some of the factors that contribute to our wellbeing are personal to us. However, there are many factors that are common to all of us, that contribute to our wellbeing. These include:

- having our biological needs for food, drink, warmth, sleep and shelter met;

- feeling safe and secure;

- having a sense of belonging and being loved and appreciated, having family, friends and good relationships in the community and with colleagues;

- having a sense of achievement and responsibility;

- being 'self actualised', which means to experience a purpose in life, realising our potential and being creative.

These needs were identified by Abraham Maslow, an important American psychologist, who wrote in the 1940s to 1960s. He developed a hierarchy of needs that we all have to satisfy before we can have a sense of wellbeing. The diagram below shows the five levels of need that Maslow identified.

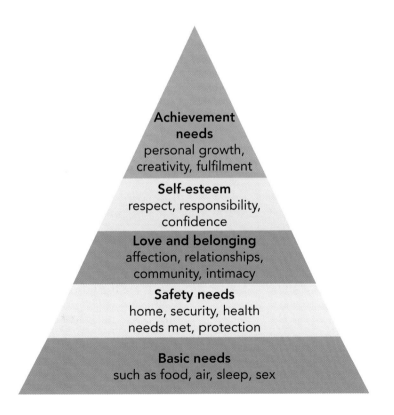

So when you are considering the factors that might contribute to a person's wellbeing you need to consider whether their needs are being met as set out on Maslow's hierarchy. In addition, once you have got to know the person you support well you will find out the particular personal things that build up their self confidence and that contribute to their wellbeing.

Activity

Think about one person you support and list the factors that contribute to their wellbeing. Think about whether Maslow's hierarchy of needs helps you to identify all the factors that contribute to their wellbeing. Discuss your ideas with your manager.

Other factors that can contribute to a person's wellbeing include:

- poor physical and mental health;

- recent experiences of bereavement or loss;

- moving home or changes in the people you live with;

- changes in personal relationships;

- losing your job or changes at work or changes in another important activity.

Also think about all of these factors when analysing what might contribute to the wellbeing of the person you support.

Key points from this chapter

- Work to make sure people have a positive self-image.

- Enable the person you support to communicate their emotional feelings as well as their practical needs.

- Make opportunities for people to belong, have close relationships and be part of their communities, and also be supported when these relationships come to an end.

- We all need times to relax, have fun and celebrate, and to be an active citizen.

References and where to go for more information

References

BILD (1998) *Exploring Your Emotions*. Kidderminster: BILD. (This book contains a useful set of photographs demonstrating emotional states or situations likely to evoke an emotional response.)

Foundation for People with Learning Disabilities (2003) *All About Feeling Down*. London: Foundation for People with Learning Disabilities

Walmsley, J and Downer, J (1997) Shouting the loudest: Self advocacy, power and diversity, in P Ramcharan, G Roberts, G Grant and J Borland, *Empowerment in Everyday Life: Learning Disability*. London: Jessica Kingsley

Websites

Books Beyond Words (a series of picture books by Sheila Hollins and colleagues, at the Royal College of Psychiatrists, covering a wide range of emotional experiences such as depression, when parents die, and personal relationships) www.rcpsych.ac.uk

Chapter 7

The role of risk assessment in enabling a person centred approach

Ben loves being with animals and enjoys taking on a helping role, so his day service arranged for him to be a volunteer at a rescue centre for abandoned pets. The day service could only provide him with transport on their minibus to go once a week, so it was decided to support Ben to take the bus there so he could increase his volunteering days. A risk assessment was completed involving Ben and with good training he soon gained confidence in catching the right bus and then walking there. He loves to get there early and make the staff a cup of coffee before they start their day. His work is really appreciated, and now he goes three days a week. Ben is really valued as part of the team, and was delighted to join the other staff and volunteers at their Christmas meal.

Luke – Ben's support worker

Learning outcomes

This chapter will help you to:

- compare different uses of risk assessment in health and social care;
- explain how risk-taking and risk assessment relate to rights and responsibilities;
- explain why risk assessments need to be regularly revised.

This chapter covers

- Level 3 HSC 036 – Implement person centred approaches in health and social care: Learning Outcome 7

Introduction

This chapter is about how we can reduce the risks associated with increased opportunities for people with a learning disability, by doing a risk assessment and planning for contingencies in case any potentially risky situations arise. This supports a person centred approach and enables people to have fulfilled and safe lives. Sometimes when we are supporting a person with a learning disability there can seem to be a conflict between our professional duty of care and their right to take the risks they choose. Because of this, in the past the support of people with learning disabilities has avoided risk. Now we know that positive risk taking, well managed and regularly reviewed, is an essential part of person centred support. It helps the person to live the life they want.

What is risk?

Risk means the likelihood of an event or circumstances occurring which can cause harm to the person involved or to other people, including all forms of abuse, neglect and exploitation.

Risk is like stress – in the right amounts it can be positive, but too much can be damaging. Life is full of risks, but we are often not even conscious of them as we subconsciously manage risky situations in everyday life, such as travelling home late at night. We often assess our own risks in terms of gain; sometimes we choose short term gain against the longer term consequence or more serious risk, such as running across a road to catch the bus. Sometimes we minimise the risk to ourselves so we can continue with certain behaviour, such as smoking.

Different approaches to risk and risk management

Past approaches to risk for people with learning disabilities

Historically, provision for many people consisted of large institutions such as hospitals or segregated village communities with everything provided on the premises. Others attended large day services where they travelled in on special coaches, and so had minimal contact with non-disabled people other than staff. People's exposure to the risks of life's experiences was carefully controlled.

Over the past few decades there have been major changes in our understanding and attitudes to people with learning disabilities and our approach to risk-taking has changed along with it. There is now greater recognition of the rights of people with learning disabilities. Like the rest of us, people with learning disabilities want the opportunity to:

- take control over their own lives;

- make their own choices and decisions;

- achieve equality and full citizenship within the society in which they live;

- determine their own futures.

By encouraging and supporting sensible and managed risk-taking we are providing the opportunity for people to experience success, deal with failure and learn from both positive and negative experiences. People will become more resilient as a result of learning from their experiences.

Risk assessment is more prevalent in some types of work settings than in others. For example, if you work with people whose behaviour challenges, risk assessment will be a regular part of your work including risk to the person, to those working with them and to others, plus the risks of undertaking certain activities or using certain approaches.

People's right to risk

As citizens, we expect certain protection from risk to be provided by the police, our legal system and regulatory bodies. We are protected against the purchase of faulty goods or from bogus doctors, for example. In law, people with learning disabilities are entitled to the same protection from risks as all of us. Equally, they should not be prevented from taking assessed and managed risks, which would deny them many potential benefits. Risk-taking is an essential element in the process of empowerment and self-determination.

The Equality and Human Rights Commission published a paper in 2009 called *From safety net to spring board*. It talks about how all care and support should be based on equality and human rights. We need to see our support to people not as a safety net preventing them from getting involved in community life and realising their dreams, but as a springboard which enables people to have more opportunities and be active and healthy.

Activity

Think about the support you have given to people – can you think of how you have been a 'springboard' so someone could enjoy their right to full life? Perhaps you gave them the motivation to try a new activity, encouraged them again to learn a new skill, spoke up for them to encourage their family to give them more freedom. If so well done! You have made a difference to someone's life.

When people do not have the opportunity to take risks

This is usually the easier option, but it is an ill-informed one. If we prevent people from taking risks, or protect them from reasonable risk-taking, or do not provide them with choice about risk-taking we:

- deny them their rights as equal and valued adults;
- deny them the right to control their own life and make their own decisions;
- deprive them of valuable and enjoyable experiences and deny new opportunities;
- reduce their ability to deal with the unforeseen risks they will inevitably encounter in life;
- prevent them learning new things or meeting new people;
- make people dependent and passive;
- ignore individual needs and differences;
- restrict lives and possibly create frustration which can lead to challenging behaviours;
- prevent them from learning from their experiences.

There is still a tendency towards over-protection today in some areas of life, such as handling money and bills, doing activities and travelling in the community and developing personal relationships. People with learning disabilities can find this stifling.

The benefits of risk taking

The benefits people who have learning disabilities can get from managed risk-taking include:

Taking acceptable risk can lead to the satisfaction of success.

- learning to identify and deal with different levels of risk;
- learning from the consequences of risk – both positive and negative;
- the satisfaction and achievement of success;
- new experiences;
- making new relationships;
- becoming better equipped to deal with life;
- growth and development as a person;
- developing independence;
- finding new opportunities for learning;
- developing better choice and decision-making skills;
- learning more advanced skills;
- enjoying an increasing variety of opportunities.

Think about a person you support and make a list of the things they do. What are the risks and benefits of what they do? For example:

Name	Activity	Risks	Benefits
Peter	Travels to college on his own on the underground.	Could be made fun of on the train. Could get lost. Might spend his lunch money on a magazine in the newsagents on the way.	He becomes more confident and can learn to travel to other places.

The tension between risk and duty of care

Everyone who works in health and social care has a duty of care to the people they support. Duty of care means that those in a professional or other paid capacity, with responsibility for providing care or support to others, must take reasonable care to avoid acts or omissions which are likely to cause harm to the person they support or to another person. Workers can be accused of negligence if they have not shown a duty of care, which is why they can be over cautious.

Duty of care may conflict with the right of the individual to take risks. Sometimes it might seem like you are walking on a tightrope between allowing choice on one side and the associated risk on the other. This doesn't mean that you should prevent people taking risks, but rather that these risks should be assessed and managed.

The book *Duty of Care for Learning Disability Workers* in this series will give you more information on duty of care and risk management.

Particular risks for people with learning disabilities

People who have a learning disability have often not been allowed or encouraged to take risks because they can be more likely to face the risk of exploitation, discrimination and abuse by others. For example:

- People who have difficulty communicating verbally are less able to tell about abuse, so are in a more vulnerable position.

- People who have difficulty understanding money are at risk of financial abuse or making simple but costly mistakes.

- People who use services are at risk of being treated unfairly, exploited, abused, being denied their rights and controlled by others.

- Some people with learning disabilities are overly trusting of people who appear to have authority over them and so are at greater risk of exploitation or abuse.

- Some people find it difficult to understand the consequences of their own actions or those of other people.

- Some people have limited experience and understanding of potential dangers.

- Some people are dependent on others for certain aspects of their lives.

- People who require help with intimate personal care are more vulnerable to abuse, both physical and sexual.

- Some people can be vulnerable if others recognise they are unlikely to report or complain, because they have limited communication or are socially isolated.

- Sometimes people are compliant with people who take advantage of them, e.g. through financial abuse, because either they do not realise it is happening, or because they are too frightened to report it or they are so lonely they put up with it because they want to keep their 'friend' – this is known as 'mate crime'.

This means people can find it hard to assess and calculate risk, and will need support in this area. However, the level of support needed usually can decrease over time as people's skills and confidence increase. This support might include enabling people to:

- be more assertive and confident;

- know how to complain;

- understand how others should treat them and what to do if they are not treated fairly;

- learn road and community safety.

Activity

What support can you give to people that will reduce risk? Think about the scenarios below. What are the risks and what would you do to manage the risk but still enable the person to have the experiences they have chosen?

- *Surrinder has epilepsy, and is going through a phase of having frequent seizures. Every day he asks if he can to go swimming.*

- *Jackie lives alone in a flat and has started inviting some local young people in as she is quite lonely. You find out from her phone bill that they have been making calls to their friends' mobiles on her phone.*

- *Diane loves one of the current boy bands and they are doing a show in town. She would love to go to see them play live but you know she shouts and screams when she gets excited and she gets upset in crowds.*

- *Lemar is very scared of dogs. He is trying to lose weight and enjoys a walk, but will run off if a dog comes near him, and he has been known to run in the road to avoid a dog even if it is on a lead.*

Relating risk taking and risk assessment to rights and responsibilities

Risk assessment

It is a legal requirement for employers to have a risk assessment policy and knowing how to use it is an important part of a support worker's role.

- Risk assessment should always be considered whenever plans are made, and should fully involve the person with a learning disability.

- The assessment should define the type and level of risk, identifying both the positive and negative consequences of an action and ways to minimise risk.

- Risk assessments should be recorded and regularly reviewed.

If a situation is complex or seen as 'high risk', it is better if a risk assessment is done as a team which includes the person and people who know the person well. The questions you need to consider relate not only to the potential risks but also to the person's rights and responsibilities. These questions include:

- What are we assessing the risk of?

- What types of risk are involved with this?

- What level of risk is there?

- What are the benefits of doing this activity?

- What rights and responsibilities are involved in this activity?

- Do the potential benefits outweigh the level of risk?

- How can we reduce the chances of risk in this activity? This involves drawing up an action plan or guidelines and might include preparation, training, strategies if things go wrong, etc.

- Does everyone agree that if the action plan and guidelines are put into place, the risk should be taken? It is good practice to ask everyone this question individually to enable everyone to communicate their personal fears or concerns based on their own knowledge of the person or the situation.

- How will the action plan and guidelines be monitored?

- When will there be a review of this risk and the strategies put in place?

Activity

Now use the risk assessment questions above to think about the risks involved in this scenario:

Carlene is going to start travelling on her own on the bus to the community lunch club for elderly people where she is a volunteer. Carlene has diabetes and is putting on weight so needs to eat the right food and take medication at lunchtime. The older ladies at the lunch club are very fond of her and try to spoil her. Some bring her sweets and they encourage her to have extra portions of pudding, which can be just too tempting.

Involving people with learning disabilities in risk assessment

As a basic principle, it is important to find ways of including the person with learning disabilities as fully as possible, and we need to find ways of doing this which suit the individual's needs and abilities.

Ensure that all records relevant to risk assessment and management are available and accessible to the person with learning disabilities, which might mean finding other ways of presenting them, for example audio-tape, simpler language, large print and using signing or symbols.

Confidentiality and risk

It is also important to be aware of the potential conflict with confidentiality when reporting assessments and decisions about risk. There are occasions when breaching confidentiality will be unavoidable but if this happens, make sure that you discuss the situation as soon as possible with your line manager.

Sample risk assessment

The example below shows how risk has been assessed and managed. It gives a numerical score to the risk – these are not essential and are subjective, but sometimes the score can help to identify where there are areas of higher risk. The control measures are things put in place to limit or reduce the risk.

A risk score 1 is low and 10 is high.

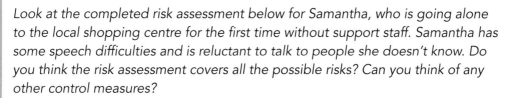

Activity

Look at the completed risk assessment below for Samantha, who is going alone to the local shopping centre for the first time without support staff. Samantha has some speech difficulties and is reluctant to talk to people she doesn't know. Do you think the risk assessment covers all the possible risks? Can you think of any other control measures?

Risk Assessment

Hazard	Risk before control measures	Likely consequences	Control measures	Risk after control measures
Getting on the wrong bus.	4	Could end up in the city centre instead.	Write the bus and direction on a small card, and ask her to show this to the driver when she gets on.	1

Spending all her money in the shops and not leaving enough to get the bus home. Very likely if she finds some jewellery she likes!	8	She will not be able to get home.	Put the return bus fare money in a sealed envelope in a pocket inside her handbag.	1
Forgetting the time and staying out past time medication is due.	6	Medication will be late.	Agree staff to call her on her mobile an hour before she is due home, to remind her to start heading back.	1
Getting disorientated in the shopping mall and getting distressed.	4	Could panic and get upset making her less confident next time.	Give Samantha another card with the on-call number on, and rehearse asking someone to show her how to get back to Joe's café, as she'll then know where she is.	2

Knowing about risk management policy and procedures

You should be familiar with your organisation's policies and procedures. This means you should:

- consider risk taking as an integral part of your work;

- be fully informed about the service's strategies for dealing with risk-taking;

- assess your day-to-day work and practice against the service's risk-taking policies and procedures;

- know where to go to for assistance in an emergency.

Activity

Find your organisation's risk assessment policy and procedures and check its accessibility for other staff and the person you support.

Check that the policy and procedures:

- *mention legal requirements in relation to risk management, including the rights and responsibilities of those involved;*

- *define the values that underlie the organisation's approach to risk;*

- *state the responsibilities of the organisation to safeguard people and minimise risk;*

- *provide clear guidance to managers and workers at all levels on their duties and responsibilities;*

- *explain how those with learning disabilities and their families and friends will know about them and be involved in the decisions.*

If you have any questions or concerns about risk assessment then talk to your manager.

Reviewing and updating risk assessments

Life is full of change – we grow older, we learn new skills, our interests diversify, we meet new friends. As we change we encounter fresh challenges and risks, and some old risks fall by the wayside. It is a reflection of our success in helping someone to lead a fuller life that frequent review and updating of risk assessment for a person is necessary.

Failure to update a risk assessment may be serious because support staff and carers could be working with a false assumption that the main risks have been identified and evaluated, and the systems in place to deal with them are still adequate. New risks may be higher and demand greater precautions, or may have declined, requiring protective measures to be downgraded. Poor practice in reviewing and updating may not only place someone at greater risk, but may also deny them the opportunities afforded by good up-to-date risk assessment.

These key areas should be regularly reviewed.

Personality

Some people have personality types which make them more likely to behave in 'risky' ways, and personality can change with factors such as time, use of medication and life events.

Physical health

With medical advances, more people with learning disabilities are living longer, but they may encounter health risks in later life which require review.

Mental health

Changes in mental health may affect the risks people present to themselves or to others. The early onset of dementia in some people with learning disabilities is an increasing and progressively changing risk factor.

Emotional wellbeing

Major losses and bereavements, including frequent moves of home and changes in care workers are often not recognised and properly resolved. The effects may emerge over many years in physical and mental ill health, changes in behaviour and relationships. Similar problems can arise as a result of isolation and boredom.

Family life

Changes affecting family life may result in situations where perceptions of risk alter too, for example, when parents divorce or a close relative dies.

Relationships

Friendships or other relationships formed may increase the chance of encountering risk, particularly where there is a strong bond between individuals, and it is important to be aware of this.

Communication skills

Communication skills may improve or decline over time which may have a direct impact on the review of risk assessments. Family carers can be asked to advise on previous strategies used to manage risk, showing them respect as equal partners.

Risk and other people

Sometimes we have to think about managing risk for other people.

Darren's mother really wants her son, who has profound and multiple learning disabilities, to go to the local youth club with his younger brother. He loves being with people and in noisy active environments but if he sees another young person with something he decides he wants, such as a table tennis bat, their crisps, or a ball he will just go and take it off people, and may scratch them in the process. How can the risks to others in this situation be managed, so that Darren can still spend an evening with his peers, and his mother has a night off to enjoy her favourite TV programmes in peace?

Unplanned risk management

We need to be aware of unexpected events leading to unplanned risk at work. Sometimes risk assessment happens in response to an emergency, as part of crisis management.

In such a situation it is important that you:

- identify the risks in the current situation;
- find ways of dealing with any adverse consequences;
- provide support to reduce the risks and negative consequences associated with them in the future;
- record and report decisions and the reasons for them;
- implement monitoring procedures so that any additional or recurring adverse consequences are dealt with immediately.

Unplanned decisions about risk and any actual or potential outcomes should be reported to your line manager and all those affected by the decision, including the person you support, if they were not involved in the decision-making.

Chantal and her support worker, Claire, went to a show in the city centre for her birthday treat. They travelled to the city centre in the support worker's car, but when they returned to the car, it wouldn't start. Claire rang the rescue service, who said it would be an hour before anyone could come out to them. Chantal doesn't cope well with unexpected routine changes and she was getting very tired and irritable and kept saying she wanted to go to bed. Claire explained that she had a choice: she could either wait or go home in a taxi on her own, something she had never done before. Chantal was certain she wanted to go home as soon as possible, so Claire decided to call a reliable taxi firm that their organisation used regularly, and Chantal travelled home alone in the taxi. Claire also rang the on-call manager to inform him of her actions, and asked the staff on duty to call her as soon as Chantal arrived back safely.

Activity

Write up a record for the scenario above, imagining you are Claire, to ensure that everyone concerned is aware of the action, who made it and why, so that appropriate follow-up action can be taken. It will also provide information for future risk assessment and safeguard you.

Key points from this chapter

- When people with a learning disability are not provided with choice and information about risk-taking or are protected from taking risks we deny them their rights, deprive them of valuable learning experiences, reduce their ability to deal with risks in the future and create a situation of inequality, dependency and disempowerment.
- Positive risk assessment and management are an essential part of person centred support.

References and where to go for more information

References

Barksby, J and Harper, L (2011) *Duty of Care for Learning Disability Workers.* Exeter: Learning Matters/BILD

Equality and Human Rights Commission (2009) *From Safety Net to Springboard,* available at www.equalityhumanrights.com

Chapter 8

Recognising possible signs of dementia

Long after I realised that this was when everything slowly began to go wrong ... from that time there were changes (in Kathleen)... Otherwise life continued with its ups and downs and then ...when she was 62, Kathleen seemed to become agitated and unlike herself.

Margaret T Fray, *Caring for Kathleen: A sister's story about Down's syndrome and dementia*

Introduction

It is important to be person centred in the support you provide for people with learning disabilities, whether they are young, middle-aged or older. In recent years, people with learning disabilities have been living much longer because of advances with medical care. One consequence of living longer is that people with a learning disability are at increased risk of illness and disease related to older age, which includes the risk of developing dementia.

Learning outcomes

This chapter will help you to:

- understand the possible signs of dementia in a person you support;

- know why depression, delirium and age-related memory impairment may be mistaken for dementia;

- understand why early diagnosis is important in relation to dementia;

- know who to tell, and how, if you suspect symptoms associated with dementia.

This chapter covers

Common Induction Standards – Standard 7 – Person centred support: Learning Outcome 3: Recognising possible signs of dementia

---

Understanding dementia

In her book, *Caring for Kathleen: A sister's story about Down's syndrome and dementia* (2000), Margaret Fray describes some of the signs she observed in her sister Kathleen over a four-year period before she was formally diagnosed with dementia. Kathleen had Down's syndrome and this made her more at risk of developing dementia in later life. Margaret observed the first signs of changes in Kathleen when she was in her mid-fifties; she was formally diagnosed when she was 62.

What is dementia?

Dementia is a general term describing a group of symptoms that are caused by changes to the brain. The damage to the brain is progressive and because brain tissue cannot be repaired or replaced the condition gets worse over time. There are a number of different types of dementia but they all include similar symptoms, such as:

- gradual loss of memory;
- a decline in thinking and reasoning skills;
- problems with communication including finding the right word and understanding what others say;
- mood and behaviour changes;
- poor sense of time and place;
- difficulties in self care and doing domestic tasks.

Although there a number of different types of dementia the main ones are:

- Alzheimer's disease – this is the most common cause of dementia. 'Plaques' or 'tangles' form in the structure of the brain and these are thought to cause the death of brain cells.
- Vascular dementia is the second most common form of dementia. Problems with the blood supply to the brain result in changes to the brain cells.

There are also other rarer forms of dementia, including Lewy bodies, Korsakoff syndrome, Binswanger's disease, etc.

There is no evidence that people with a learning disability are affected differently by dementia, but there is evidence that the prevalence of dementia in people with learning disability generally and people with Down's syndrome in particular is higher than in the general population.

Between 15 and 20 per cent of people with a learning disability have Down's syndrome, and they are at a higher risk of developing Alzheimer's disease. Studies have shown that almost all people with Down's syndrome develop the plaques and tangles in their brain associated with Alzheimer's disease although not everyone will develop the symptoms. Prevalence increases with age in people with Down's syndrome.

For people with other forms of learning disability not associated with Down's syndrome the prevalence of dementia is also higher than in the general population. People with a learning disability not related to Down's syndrome are four times more likely than the general population to get dementia, that is 13 per cent of people over 50 years and 22 per cent of people 65 years and over. At present the reasons for this increase in the numbers of people with a learning disability being diagnosed with dementia are unknown, and further research is needed.

(Information taken from the Alzheimer's society factsheet, *Learning Disabilities and Dementia*, available at www.alzheimers.org.uk)

The possible signs of dementia

In their book, *Down's Syndrome and Dementia: A resource for carers and support staff* (2009), Karen Dodd and her colleagues Vicky Turk and Michelle Christmas say that it is helpful to think about the changes that occur for a person with any type of dementia in three main stages: early, middle and late. The symptoms listed below are the most frequently occurring for each stage. However, it is always important to remember that all individuals are different and each person will show a unique pattern through the stages below. Progression of the dementia varies considerably from person to person.

Early stage dementia can include:

- loss of short term memory;
- language problems - finding the right words;
- deteriorating performance on usual tasks;
- changes in behaviour;
- disorientation.

Middle stage dementia can include:

- symptoms becoming more obvious, particularly language skills;
- disorientation in time, place and person;
- confusion resulting in frustration;
- loss of self care skills including continence;
- long periods of inactivity or apathy;
- more severe changes in personality and social behaviour.

Late stage dementia can include:

- loss of eating and drinking skills;
- problems with mobility;
- problems with recognising people;
- development of seizures;
- often needing 24-hour care;
- increases in general health problems, e.g. pressure sores, infections etc.

Support workers, family and friends are important in helping to identify dementia. Because they know the person best they are often the first to notice changes in health, communication and behaviour.

Other conditions which may be mistaken for dementia

There are many conditions that can cause a person with a learning disability to show one or more of the symptoms of dementia. For example:

- thyroid problems;
- urinary tract infections;
- depression and other mental health problems;
- a sensory loss;
- the effect of medication;
- age-related memory impairment.

So before jumping to a hasty conclusion that the person might be showing the signs of dementia you need to think more widely about the full range of reasons a person might be showing certain symptoms. This is because one or more of the symptoms of dementia may be present but this doesn't mean the person has dementia.

As a support worker who works closely with a person with a learning disability on a day-to-day basis you are in a key position to contribute to understanding the reasons behind a person's changes in behaviour. Others who know the person well, their family and close friends may similarly notice early changes. Your observations and your recording of these changes will be helpful in assisting a doctor to make a diagnosis.

There is no single assessment that a doctor can use to diagnose dementia. Instead they will use a number of tools, including:

- taking a detailed personal history – to understand the types of changes the person is experiencing;

- doing a full health assessment;

- assessing the person's psychological state;

- undertaking any special investigations as required, for example a brain scan.

When diagnosing people with a learning disability some of the standard cognitive tests may need to be changed or adapted as they require the person to use some complex skills involving language or understanding they may not have. New tests are being developed that may be done with a specialist professional such as a psychologist or psychiatrist or a learning disability nurse.

Understanding why early diagnosis is important

For many of us when we feel unwell and are unsure about what is wrong with us it is often very helpful to get a proper diagnosis from a doctor. Not only does this stop us worrying and imagining all sorts of possible diseases or illnesses, it also means we can find out more and explore different treatments with our doctor. For many illnesses, getting an early diagnosis means we can get treatment to either cure our illness or to slow down its progression if it is an incurable illness.

Currently there is no cure for dementia but there are drugs and other interventions that can help to slow down the rate of progress of the disease. So getting an early diagnosis could help the person you support in a number of ways:

1. It will help them and those who love and support them to understand the changes they have been experiencing.

2. It will help them explore possible treatments with their doctor.

3. It will help them and those who support them to plan for when the disease progresses so that support can remain person centred and adapt to the person's changing needs.

4. Once a diagnosis of dementia has been made, the people and organisation that support the person can plan both for the person to receive good support now, but also plan for when their needs change.

5. Later the person can be given support with an end of life plan so that they can receive person centred care to the end of their life.

If the person you support gets an early diagnosis of dementia they may well carry on their life and activities in much the same way for some time. Supporting them to maintain their skills for as long as possible is important so that the person has a good quality of life. Eventually the person's plan and their support will have to change and adapt to their changing needs.

Knowing who to tell, and how

If you are working with a person with a learning disability and you are concerned that they may be showing some of the signs of dementia what should you do?

Remember that the person's doctor is the right person to give a formal diagnosis. However, you have important role to play in identifying and reporting changes in behaviour and highlighting your concerns. The list below gives some examples of what you should do if you have concerns about changes in the health and behaviour of the person you support, regardless of whether or not these are related to possible signs of dementia.

- Make notes of your specific concerns in the person's care plan or the handover book. Be factual and specific in what you write. You don't need to add your own ideas and opinions about what might be happening. For example:

  - Greg forgot the route we always take when we walk the dog again today. When he got to the junction at the end of the road he stood looking confused and anxious. He couldn't remember that we always turn left down Wall Lane and into the park. This is the third time this has happened in the last week. ✓

  - Greg's getting confused again. I think he is losing it, not knowing where he is going when we walk the dog. ✗

– Greg is still finding it difficult to get dressed in the morning. In the past he could dress himself independently with just a little help with small buttons and zips. Now he is putting on cardigans and jumpers back to front or inside out. Last year this never happened but now he has problems like this 3–4 times per week. ✓

– Greg getting so slow and muddled these days, such a problem dressing I have to help most days now! ✗

- If possible ask the person how they are feeling, and if they raise concerns about their health work with them to arrange a visit to their GP.

- Talk to your manager and others who know the person well, such as members of their family or close friends, about the specific changes you have observed and reported.

- If the person receives support from the community learning disability team or a specialist learning disability nurse you could discuss your concerns with them.

People with learning disabilities who think they may be unwell or experiencing signs of dementia should go to their family doctor, who will assess their health needs.

Key points from this chapter

- People with dementia will increasingly lose their memory and their skills.

- This means their behaviour at times will change too as they become frustrated, anxious and depressed.

- Your support needs to reflect these changes and you will increasingly need to support the person practically and emotionally.

- It is important that people the person might meet in other settings are also aware of these changes.

- You can also be creative and try and make life easier by using reminders on calendars, naming people on photos, labelling drawers, etc.

References and where to go for further information

References

Alzheimer's Society (2010) *Learning Disabilities and Dementia*, Factsheet 430, available at www.alzheimers.org.uk

Care Quality Commission (2010) *Best Practice in Mental Health Services for People with a Learning Disability (green light toolkit)*, available at www.cqc.org.uk

Dodd, K, Turk, V, Christmas, M (2009) *Down's Syndrome and Dementia: A resource for carers and support staff* (second edition). Kidderminster: BILD

Flintshire County Council (2009) *Dementia and People with Learning Disabilities: Information for carers*, available at www.siryfflint.gov.uk

Fray, M (2000) *Caring for Kathleen: A sister's story about Down's syndrome and dementia*. Kidderminster: BILD

Websites

Clear Thoughts: the mental health in learning disability knowledge centre (a website for people with a learning disability and people who support them on mental health issues) www.clearthoughts.info

Glossary

Advocacy – helping and supporting someone to speak up for what they want.

Age appropriate – means the communication or activity should be right for the age of the person who you support.

Code of conduct – a document provided by an organisation setting out the standards that staff are expected to work to.

Code of practice – a UK document for social care workers setting out the standards they should work to.

Communication – the way that two or more people make contact, build relationships and share messages. These messages can be ideas, thoughts or feelings as well as information and questions. Communication involves both sending and understanding these messages and can be done through many different ways including speech, writing, drawing, pictures, symbols, signs, pointing and body language, for example.

Complaint – any expression of unhappiness, whether spoken or written, from or on behalf of a person about a service's provision of, or failure to provide, care and support.

Confidentiality – making sure that information is kept private and is only shared with authorised people on a need to know basis.

Consent – a person consents if he or she agrees by choice and has the freedom and capacity to make that choice.

Direct payments – a way for people to organise their own social care support by receiving funding direct from their council following an assessment of their needs.

Duty of care – a professional responsibility to act in the best interest of the person receiving support or care.

Empower – enabling an individual to think, behave, take action, and control work and decision making independently.

Family carer – a relative of a person with learning disabilities who has an interest in their wellbeing.

General Social Care Council – the organisation that regulates the social care workforce in England and sets the standards of care through the Code of Practice.

Legislation – laws introduced by the government that set out people's rights and also how health and social care services should be provided.

Mental capacity – a person's ability to make their own decisions and to understand the consequences of those decisions.

Models of disability – how we see the place of people with disabilities in society and how we respond to them.

Person centred approaches – this term covers a range of approaches to individual planning that are led by people who need support such as people with learning disabilities and their families and friends.

Person centred planning – a structured way to make sure that people with learning disabilities are at the centre of all planning, choices and discussions about their life. Person centred planning helps them to live their lives in their own way and to meet their wishes and dreams.

Personal assistants – a term often used to describe people employed directly by a person to provide care and support (e.g. through direct payments or an individual budget).

Personalisation – starting with the person as an individual with strengths, preferences and aspirations and putting them at the centre of the process of identifying their needs and making choices about how and when they are supported to live their lives.

Policy – a statement or plan of action that clearly sets out an organisation's position or approach on a particular issue and tells staff what should be done in the circumstances.

Power – the ability of a person or group of people to exercise authority over another, thereby controlling and influencing others.

Procedure – a set of instructions that sets out in detail how a policy should be put into practice and what staff should do in response to a specific situation.

Public services – services which the government provides such as social services, hospitals and schools.

Reflection – careful consideration of ideas and issues.

Rights – a framework of laws that protects people from harm, sets out what people can say and do and guarantees the right to a fair trial and other basic entitlements, such as the right to respect, equality, etc.

Risk – probability or threat of damage, injury, liability, loss, or other negative occurrence which may be prevented through planned action.

Risk assessment – a careful examination of what could cause harm to people, so that you can weigh up whether you have taken enough precautions or should do more to prevent harm.

Safeguarding – helping to protect vulnerable people from abuse by others.

Social inclusion – when individuals with a learning disability are included and involved in everyday life, and so have the same life chances as other members of society regardless of their learning disability.

Staff – people employed on a paid or unpaid (voluntary) basis by an organisation to organise and deliver its services.

Support plan – detailed plan of a person's support needs that support workers should use to inform their day-to-day support for that individual.

Vulnerable adult – a person who is or may be in need of community care services by reason of mental or other disability, age or illness and who is or may be unable to take care of themselves against significant harm or exploitation.

Whistleblower – someone who reports wrongdoing or bad practices to higher authorities.

Index

Added to a page number 'g' denotes glossary.